MW01224950

Language Launch

Volume 1

UNIT 2 | Getting to Know You

Printed in the U.S.A.

ISBN   978-0-358-86409-7

r12.23

3 4 5 6 7 8 9 10   0607   32 31 30 29 28 27 26 25 24

4500885123

Table of Contents

Unit 2

Unit 2: Getting to Know You

 Make Observations

Look at the image. Discuss what you see.

Draw or take notes to help you.

Meet Santiago!

Santiago is your host for Unit 2: Getting to Know You. He will guide you through the unit by giving you helpful information!

What is your favorite part of your new school?

My new friends are my favorite part of school. We have so much fun in school and after school too!

How did you make friends?

I made friends by getting to know my classmates during lunch.

What do you like to do after school?

I like to watch movies and skateboard after school.

What are all of your languages?

I speak and write in both Spanish and English.

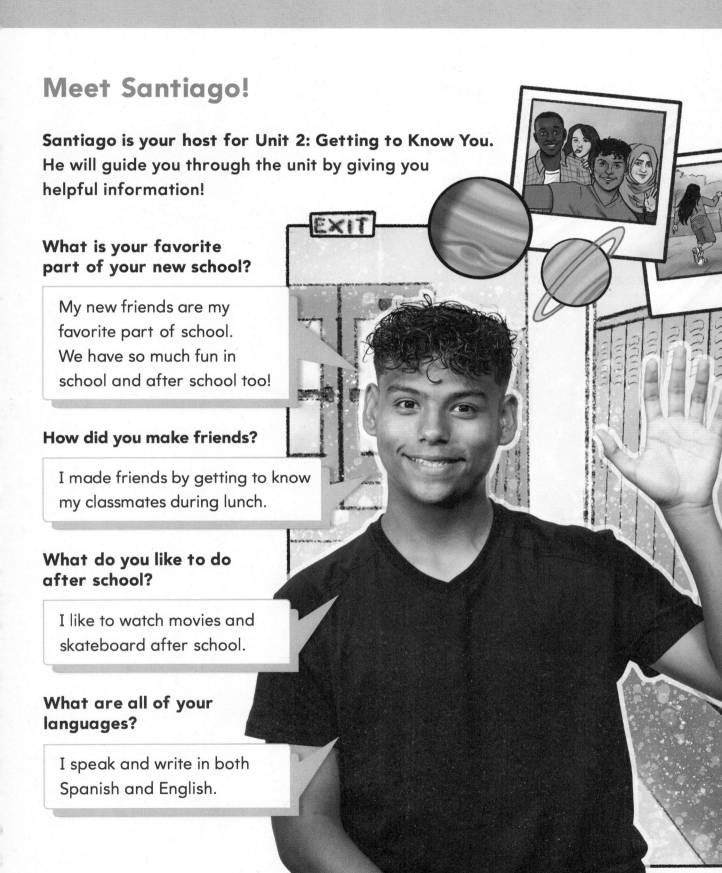

View the Anchor Video

One way to make new friends is by getting to know what they like to do! Let's watch a video to learn more about making friends.

 Vocabulary Builder

1. Say It   **2.** See It   **3.** Read It   **4.** Write It

feel

feel
(verb)

Santiago **feels** nervous on his first day of school.

Word _____
    feel

Translation _____

Make Connections _____

_____

like

like
(verb)

Haja **likes** to play the drums.

Word _____
    like

Translation _____

Make Connections _____

_____

together

to • **geth** • er
(adverb)

We eat lunch **together** almost every day.

Word _____
   together

Translation _____

Make Connections _____

_____

try

try
(verb)

Arepas   Dolma

Santiago and Haja like to **try** new foods.

Word _____
   try

Translation _____

Make Connections _____

_____

Vocabulary Review

feel   together

like   try

Share translations with a partner.

LANGUAGE TO
SHARE TRANSLATIONS 💬

What language do you speak?

I speak (language).

· ·

Can you share a word in (language)?

The (language) word for _____ is _____.

Arepas

Dolma

Complete each sentence. Then rewrite each sentence.

1. I **like** to _____ .
(verb phrase)

_____

_____

2. I want to **try** to _____ .
(verb phrase)

_____

_____

LANGUAGE TO
SHARE IDEAS

What did you write?

I wrote _____ .

View the Anchor Video

Characters

Characters are the people in a story.

Watch the video again. Look and listen for the four characters and how they met each other.

 ## Review Characters

Write the name of each character under the correct image.

_____

_____

_____

_____

| Chen | Erick | Haja | Santiago |

Respond to Multimedia

Complete the sentences with details from the video.

Model: How did Santiago feel on his first day of school?

Santiago felt _____nervous_____ on his first day of school.
(nervous/excited/happy)

1. When did Santiago meet his friend Chen?

   Santiago met his friend Chen on the _____
   (first/second/last)
   day of school.

2. Where did Santiago meet his friend Haja?

   Santiago met his friend Haja at _____.
   (lunch/breakfast/soccer practice)

3. Where did Santiago meet his friend Erick?

   Santiago met his friend Erick in _____ class.
   (science/social studies/math)

4. What did Santiago try to do?

   Santiago tried to _____.
   (play the drums/watch a movie/read a book)

LANGUAGE TO COLLABORATE 💬

What can we choose?

We can choose _____.

Vocabulary and Language

 View the Anchor Video

Watch the video again. Listen and look
for the things each character likes to do.

 Vocabulary Builder

1. Say It **2.** See It **3.** Read It **4.** Write It

interest

in • ter • est
(noun)

An **interest** is an activity you like to do or a topic you want to
learn more about. One of Chen's **interests** is skateboarding.

Word _____
　　　　　interest

Translation _____

Make Connections _____

_____

talent

tal • ent
(noun)

A **talent** is an activity you are good at. Santiago's **talent**
is doing science experiments.

Word _____
　　　　　talent

Translation _____

Make Connections _____

_____

similar

sim • i • lar
(adjective)

Santiago and Erick are **similar** because they both like to do science experiments.

Word _____
similar

Translation _____

Make Connections _____

_____

different

dif • fer • ent
(adjective)

Santiago and Haja are **different** because she likes to play the drums and he likes science.

Word _____
different

Translation _____

Make Connections _____

_____

Vocabulary and Language

 Vocabulary Review

interest

similar

talent

different

Share translations with a partner.

LANGUAGE TO **SHARE TRANSLATIONS**
What language do you speak?   I speak (<u>language</u>).   ....   Can you share a word in (<u>language</u>)?   The (<u>language</u>) word for _____ is _____.

Complete each sentence.

1. I am good at playing the violin. My friend is good at singing. We have

   _____ _____ .
   (similar/different)   *(interests/talents)*

2. My friend and I both like music. We have a _____
                                              (similar/different)

   _____ .
   (interest/talent)

3. I like music and I also like sports. I have many _____
                                                    (similar/different)

   _____ .
   (interests/talents)

LANGUAGE TO
SHARE IDEAS

What did you write?

I wrote ____ .

View and Take Notes

Watch the video again. Listen for the characters' interests, or things that the characters like to do.

Take notes on each character's interests.

Character	Likes to...
Santiago	
Chen	
Haja	
Erick	

Write About It

Complete the sentences to tell how the characters in the video are similar and different.

Model: Santiago is _____similar to_____ Chen because they both like to skateboard.
(similar to/different from)

1. Santiago is _____ Haja because they both like to try new foods.
(similar to/different from)

2. Santiago is _____ Haja because he likes to do science
(similar to/different from)

   experiments, but she likes to _____.
   (interest)

3. Santiago is _____ Eric because they both like
(similar to/different from)

   to _____.
   (interest)

Make Connections

Partner A, **ask questions.** Partner B, **respond.** Then switch roles.

A: What do you like to do on the weekend?

B: On the weekend, I like to _____.
(interest)

A: What do you like to do after school?

B: After school, I like to _____.
(interest)

WORD BANK

Interests

do science experiments	play basketball
draw pictures	play the drums
learn new languages	read books
listen to music	try new foods
make videos	watch movies

_____

_____

Thanks for watching! Now let's learn more about sharing your interests and what makes you *YOU*!

You Can Call Me . . .

My name is Santiago! What's your name?
Let's learn words to talk about our names!

 Vocabulary Builder

1. Say It   **2.** See It   **3.** Read It   **4.** Write It

---

call

call
(verb)

He said that everyone can **call** him Giovani or Gio.

Word _____
      call

Translation _____

Make Connections _____

_____

---

last name

last name
(noun)

Giovani Dominguez

Giovani Dominguez is his full name. Dominguez is his **last name**.

Word _____
      last name

Translation _____

Make Connections _____

_____

nickname

nick • name
(noun)

Giovani
↓
Gio

A **nickname** is another name some people have.
Giovani's **nickname** is Gio.

Word _____
        nickname

Translation _____

Make Connections _____

_____

---

pronounce

pro • **nounce**
(verb)

**Giovani
(Gee-o-von-ee)**

When you **pronounce** a word, you sound out the letters.
Giovani is **pronounced** *Gee-o-von-ee*.

Word _____
        pronounce

Translation _____

Make Connections _____

_____

---

correct

cor • **rect**
(adjective)

Giovani ✓
Govani

When a word is **correct**, it is spelled with all the right letters.
The **correct** way to spell Giovani is G-i-o-v-a-n-i.

Word _____
        correct

Translation _____

Make Connections _____

_____

wrong

wrong
(adjective)

Giovani
Govani ✗

Giovani's name is spelled **wrong**. It is missing the letter *i*.

Word _____
       wrong

Translation _____

Make Connections _____

_____

remember

re • **mem** • ber
(verb)

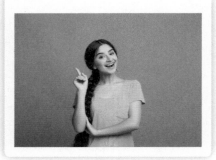

When you **remember** something, you think of it again.

Word _____
      remember

Translation _____

Make Connections _____

_____

forget

for • **get**
(verb)

Try not to **forget** a new friend's name!

Word _____
      forget

Translation _____

Make Connections _____

_____

Vocabulary Review

| call | nickname | correct | remember |

| last name | pronounce | wrong | forget |

Share translations with a partner.

LANGUAGE TO SHARE TRANSLATIONS

What language do you speak?

I speak (language).

· ·

Can you share a word in (language)?

The (language) word for _____ is _____.

Write sentences about your name.

1. My **last name** is _____.

2. My **nickname** is _____.

   I don't have a _____.

LANGUAGE TO SHARE IDEAS

What did you write?

I wrote _____.

Language Builder

Possessive Adjectives

A **possessive adjective** tells who a noun belongs to. Look for a <u>subject pronoun</u> to help you choose the correct possessive adjective.

Subject Pronoun	Possessive Adjective
I	my
you	your
he	his
she	her
it	its
we	our
they	their

Use **my** for something that belongs to you.

*<u>I</u> am Anaís. **My** name is Anaís.*

Use **your** for something that belongs to the person you are speaking to.

*Nice to meet <u>you</u>. What is **your** name?*

Use **our** for something that belongs to a group that you are a part of.

*<u>We</u> are the Mendozas. **Our** last name is Mendoza.*

Use **his**, **her**, or **their** for things that belong to other people.

*<u>He</u> is Mamoud. **His** name is Mamoud.*
*<u>She</u> is Aasha. **Her** name is Aasha.*
*<u>They</u> are Azari. **Their** name is Azari.*
*<u>They</u> are sisters. **Their** last name is Cato.*

Write the correct possessive adjective to complete each sentence.

Model: We have a dog. _____Our_____ dog's name is Buddy.
                              (Possessive Adjective)

1. She is a teacher. _____ name is Ms. Garrick.
                      (Possessive Adjective)

2. I have a friend named Jake. _____ friend's name is Jake.
                                (Possessive Adjective)

3. It's nice to meet you. What is _____ name?
                                  (possessive adjective)

4. They are brothers. _____ last name is Jean-Pierre.
                       (Possessive Adjective)

5. We play on a baseball team. _____ team's name is the Wildcats.
                               (Possessive Adjective)

LANGUAGE TO COMPARE

I wrote that too.

I wrote the same answer.

Listen Up

Listen to the conversation.

 Hi! My name is Christian. It's pronounced CHRIS-TIAN.

Cool! What should I call you?

You can call me Chris! It's pronounced CHRIS.

Thanks, Chris!

Talk About It

Partner A, ask questions. Partner B, respond. Then switch roles.

A: Hi! My name is _____.

(Name)

It's pronounced _____.

(pronunciation)

B: Cool! What should I call you?

A: You can call me _____.

(Name or Nickname)

It's pronounced _____.

(pronunciation)

B: Thanks, _____!

(Name)

Text Type: Realistic Fiction

A **story** that is **realistic fiction** has **characters**, **places**, and **events**. The story is made up, but it could happen in real life.

"The Girl Who Could Be King"
from *Ways to Make Sunshine*
by Renée Watson

1   I am a girl with a name that a lot of boys have. So when the **substitute teacher** takes **roll** and calls out, "Ryan?" she looks surprised when I answer. I wish Ms. Colby were here. Ms. Colby doesn't even need to take roll anymore because it is the first day of March and she's been teaching us for six months, so she can tell who is here and who is not just by looking across the room. Ms. Colby always starts the day off with our Thumbs-Up/Thumbs-Down/Somewhere-in-the-Middle Check-In. This substitute teacher doesn't do any of that and so I don't get to show my thumbs-up for making perfect scrambled eggs and toast this morning.

2   I wonder why Ms. Colby didn't leave a note for the sub with a list of do's and don'ts. Like don't **call** DeVonté, DeVonté—**call** him D. And don't look so **shocked** when a girl raises her hand when you call out for Ryan.

3   "Here," I say.

4   "Ryan Hart?" the substitute says. She looks at me like she is not sure I am who I say I am.

5   "Yes. My name is Ryan."

6   "Oh," she says, pushing up her too-big glasses.

7   Brandon, the boy sitting next to me, says, "She has a boy's name."

8   I roll my eyes at him because no one is talking to him and he needs to mind his own business. "I do not have a boy's name. I have my name.

My name is Ryan and Ryan means 'king' and that means I am a **leader**—"

9   "Okay, ah, please settle down. Settle down," the substitute teacher says, mostly to me and not to Brandon, who thinks he knows it all. "Okay, Ryan Hart is here," she says to herself.

10   Then Brandon whispers, "And she spells her **last name** wrong." He laughs at his corny joke.

Glossary

··

substitute teacher (noun)
A **substitute teacher** is your teacher when your regular teacher is absent, or not in school that day.

roll (noun)
Roll is another word for attendance. When a teacher takes roll, the teacher calls each student's name to see who is in class.

shocked (adjective)
When you are **shocked**, you are surprised by something you did not expect.

leader (noun)
A **leader** is a person who others follow and want to be like.

11   "I do not! My name is Ryan Hart and it's not heart like the muscle, it's H-A-R-T as in . . . as in my **last name**."

12   The substitute teacher walks over to my desk and says, "I need you to keep your voice down."

13   "I need Brandon to leave me alone!" I roll my eyes at Brandon again, extra roll this time, but then I **remember** what Mom always tells me, how she named me Ryan because she wanted me to feel **powerful**, to **remember** that I am a leader every time someone calls my name. Dad is always telling me our people come from royalty, that my ancestors lived in Africa and were kings and queens and inventors and hard workers. Mom tells me their strength is running through my veins.

14   I sit up straight, **ignore** Brandon, and try to be the leader I am supposed to be.

15   Mom and Dad tell me I will keep **growing into** my name. They say it to my brother, too. "Be who we named you to be," they tell him whenever he is pulling my ponytail or grabbing food off my plate when I'm not looking.

16   My brother's name is Raymond. We **call** him Ray. His name means "protector" and Dad says he should be keeping me, his little sister, safe. But mostly he is just **bossy** and nosy and sometimes he treats me like I am a glass thing that could break. He is always telling me *you can't do this* and *you shouldn't be so that*.

17   Maybe because I am two years younger than him, maybe because I am a girl. Maybe because he doesn't know the meaning of my name, how tough I really am.

18   Maybe he doesn't realize I can do and be anything.

Glossary

....

powerful (adjective)
When you feel **powerful**, you feel strong and important.

ignore (verb)
When you **ignore** someone, you stop speaking and listening to them.

grow into (verb)
When you **grow into** something, it fits or becomes right over time.

bossy (adjective)
Someone who is **bossy** tells other people what to do, even when they should not.

Take notes on the story.

_____

_____

_____

_____

_____

LANGUAGE TO REACT

What is one word you would use to describe the story?
One word I would use to describe the story is _____.

....

What question do you have about the story?
One question I have is: _____?

Read and Respond

> ### Characters
>
> The **characters** are the **people** in a story. The **main character** is the most important person in the story.

Read the story again. <u>Underline</u> the names of characters. Highlight the main character's name.

Match each character's name with how the character knows Ryan.

Ray	is her teacher.
Brandon	is her classmate who is called D.
Ms. Colby	is her brother.
DeVonté	is her classmate who bothers her.

Answer the questions about the text.

1. Reread paragraph 8.

   I roll my eyes at him because no one is talking to him and he needs to mind his own business. "I do not have a boy's name. I have my name. My name is Ryan and Ryan means 'king' and that means I am a leader—"

   What do we learn about Ryan's name?

   (a) We learn that her name means "king."

   (b) We learn that she does not like her name.

   (c) We learn that her name is often mispronounced.

2. Reread paragraph 13.

   "I need Brandon to leave me alone!" I roll my eyes at Brandon again, extra roll this time, but then I remember what Mom always tells me, how she named me Ryan because she wanted me to feel powerful, to remember that I am a leader every time someone calls my name. Dad is always telling me our people come from royalty, that my ancestors lived in Africa and were kings and queens and inventors and hard workers. Mom tells me their strength is running through my veins.

   What does Ryan try to remember when someone calls her name?

   (a) She is a Hart.

   (b) She is a leader.

   (c) She is a student.

Write About It

> **Don't forget!**
>
> A **possessive** adjective tells who something belongs to.
>
> *Her* name is Ms. Dixon. **His** name is Trey.

Write together. Write about your teacher.

Model: Let me introduce you to my teacher. <u>Her</u> name is <u>Gilda Herrera</u>. I call <u>her</u> <u>Mrs. Herrera</u>. <u>Mrs. Herrera</u> likes to <u>read books</u> and <u>listen to salsa music</u>.

Let me introduce you to my teacher. _____ name is
(Her/His/Their)

_____.
(Name)

I call _____ _____.
    (her/him/them)   *(Name or Nickname)*

_____ likes to _____
(Name or Nickname)   *(verb phrase)*

and _____.
  (verb phrase)

WORD BANK

Nouns (people)	**Possessive Adjectives**	**Pronouns**	**Verb Phrases (action phrases)**
brother sister	her	her	help me
favorite teacher character	his	him	listen to music
friend	their	them	play sports
			read books

Write by yourself. Write about someone you know or your favorite character.

Model: Let me introduce you to my <u>brother</u>. <u>His</u> name is <u>William</u>. I call <u>him</u> <u>Will</u>. <u>Will</u> likes to <u>read comic books</u> and <u>play video games</u>.

Let me introduce you to my _____.
                                  (noun)

_____ name is _____.
(Her/His/Their)   (Name)

I call _____ _____.
        (her/him/them)   (Name or Nickname)

_____ likes to _____.
(Name or Nickname)   (verb phrase)

and _____.
      (verb phrase)

Great work! Now you can talk about your name.
Tell your partner your name and what you like to do:
*My name is (Name). You can call me (Name or Nickname).
I like to (verb phrase).*

My Strengths

We all have strengths, or things we are good at.
For example, some people are friendly. They say hello
to new friends. Let's learn how to talk about our strengths.

 Vocabulary Builder

1. Say It **2.** See It **3.** Read It **4.** Write It

brave
brave
(adjective)

He is **brave** to present in front of the class.

Word _____
    brave

Translation _____

Make Connections _____

_____

collaborative
col • **lab** • o • ra • **tive**
(adjective)

We are **collaborative** and like working together.

Word _____
    collaborative

Translation _____

Make Connections _____

_____

curious

cu • ri • ous
(adjective)

He is **curious** about the birds. He wants to learn more about them.

Word _____
curious

Translation _____

Make Connections _____

_____

honest

hon • est
(adjective)

Good friends are **honest** with each other and do not lie.

Word _____
honest

Translation _____

Make Connections _____

_____

imaginative

i • **mag** • i • na • tive
(adjective)

She is **imaginative** and thinks about things in new ways!

Word _____
imaginative

Translation _____

Make Connections _____

_____

kind

kind
(adjective)

He is **kind** and helps other people.

Word _____
　　　kind

Translation _____

Make Connections _____

_____

responsible

re • **spon** • si • ble
(adjective)

Mila is a **responsible** older sister.

Word _____
　　　responsible

Translation _____

Make Connections _____

_____

studious

stu • di • ous
(adjective)

I am **studious** and do my homework every night.

Word _____
　　　studious

Translation _____

Make Connections _____

_____

Vocabulary Review

brave	curious	imaginative	responsible
collaborative	honest	kind	studious

Share translations with a partner.

LANGUAGE TO SHARE TRANSLATIONS

What language do you speak?

I speak (language).

Can you share a word in (language)?

The (language) word for _____ is _____.

Write sentences using new vocabulary.

1. I am **kind** because I _____
  (verb phrase)

  _____.

2. I am **responsible** because I _____
  (verb phrase)

  _____.

WORD BANK

Verb Phrases (action phrases)

clean up after eating lunch

help new students

do my chores

listen to my friends' problems

_____

LANGUAGE TO COMPARE

I wrote that too.

I wrote the same answer.

Language Builder

Verb: *to be*

Use the **verb *to be*** to connect a <u>subject</u> to an adjective that describes the subject.

<u>I</u> **am** brave.
<u>The student</u> **is** brave.
<u>The students</u> **are** brave.

The **verb *to be*** changes form to match the <u>subject</u>.

<u>I</u> **am** brave.
<u>You</u> **are** brave.
<u>He/She/It</u> **is** brave.
<u>We</u> **are** brave.
<u>They</u> **are** brave.

Highlight the form of the verb *to be*. **<u>Underline</u>** the subject.

Model: <u>I</u> am honest.

1. He is kind because he helps his neighbor.

2. They are honest and do not cheat at sports.

3. I am collaborative and work well in small groups.

4. She is studious and does her homework every night.

5. We are imaginative and have great ideas.

LANGUAGE TO SHARE IDEAS

What did you highlight?
I highlighted the verb
_____.

· ·

What did you underline?
I underlined the subject
_____.

💡 **Don't forget!**

The **verb *to be*** changes form to match the subject, which can be a noun or a pronoun.

I **am** _____.   We **are** _____.

You **are** _____.   They **are** _____.

He/She/It **is** _____.

Write the correct form of *to be* to complete each sentence.

Model: He ____is____ friendly to new students.

1. I _____ helpful when someone needs directions.

2. They _____ athletic and play soccer.

3. We _____ musical, and we play in a band.

4. She _____ curious about coding video games.

5. He _____ a responsible student.

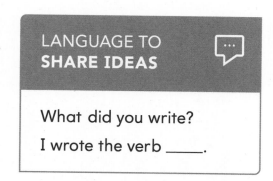

LANGUAGE TO
SHARE IDEAS

What did you write?

I wrote the verb _____.

Listen Up

Listen to the conversation.

> ▶ Hi, Mateo! What is one of your strengths?

> Hello, Serene! I am brave.

> That's great! What are some of your other strengths?

> I am honest. I am also responsible.

Talk About It

Partner A, ask questions. Partner B, respond. Then switch roles.

A: Hi, _____!
    (Name)

What is one of your strengths?

B: Hello, _____!
    (Name)

I am _____.
    (adjective)

A: That's great! What are some of your other strengths?

B: I am _____.
    (adjective)

I am also _____.
    (adjective)

WORD BANK ✦

Adjectives (describing words)

brave	honest	responsible
collaborative	imaginative	studious
curious	kind	

Functional Text: Application

An **application** is a form you complete to apply for something, like a job or a club.

The **applicant** is the person who fills out the application.

An application includes **information** about the applicant. It tells why they should be selected.

The applicant **submits** the application to a person or group.

Student Council Application

Name: Kaj Phang   **Grade:** 11th Grade

Email: K.Phang@school.com

Student council members help make our school a great place! Members meet once a week. They share ideas for making our school better. They work together to make those ideas happen.

Part A: Which topic is most important to you? Underline one.

school lunches	school clubs	job training
recycling	arts in school	tutoring

Part B: Describe three of your strengths.

1. I am studious. I do my homework every day.

2. I am also imaginative. I have great ideas about how to recycle more at school.

3. In addition, I am responsible. I will attend all meetings.

Read and Respond

Read the student council application and take notes. Then answer the questions.

LANGUAGE TO SHARE IDEAS

What did you write?

I wrote _____.

Name: _____

Important Topic: _____

Strengths: _____

_____

1. Why did Kaj Phang fill out the application?

   (a) She wants a job.

   (b) She wants to be a tutor.

   (c) She wants to be on the student council.

2. Kaj Phang says she does homework every day. This shows she is _____.

   (a) brave

   (b) collaborative

   (c) studious

3. Evaluate Kaj Phang's application. Do you think she should be on the student council? Tell why.

   I think Kaj Phang _____ be on the
                                                    (should/should not)

   student council because she is _____.
                                                          (adjective)

Write About It

 Remember!

Use **am**, a form of the **verb *to be***, to describe yourself.

*I **am** friendly to new students.*

Write a paragraph to describe your strengths.

Model: I have many strengths. I <u>am kind</u> because I <u>help people</u>. Also, I <u>am honest</u> because I <u>do not lie</u>. Finally, I <u>am curious</u> because I <u>want to learn more</u>.

I have many strengths. I _____
                                                       (am + adjective)

because I _____
              (verb phrase)

_____.

Also, I _____
               (am + adjective)

because I _____
              (verb phrase)

_____.

Finally, I _____
               (am + adjective)

because I _____
              (verb phrase)

_____.

WORD BANK

Adjectives (describing words)	Verb Phrases (action phrases)
brave	do not lie
collaborative	do things that scare me
curious	do what I say I will
honest	help people
imaginative	like to work with others
kind	study a lot
responsible	think of great ideas
studious	want to know things

LANGUAGE TO REACT

I learned _____.

I also learned _____.

Terrific! Now you can talk about your strengths.
Tell your partner two of your strengths: *I am
(adjective). I am also (adjective).*

Save the Date

A calendar shows the dates of when things happen. Let's learn how to talk about dates on the calendar.

 ## Vocabulary Builder

1. Say It   **2.** See It   **3.** Read It   **4.** Write It

calendar

cal • en • dar
(noun)

I write events on the **calendar** to know when they happen.

Word _____
        calendar

Translation _____

Make Connections _____

_____

year

year
(noun)

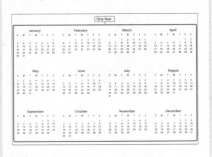

There are 365 days in a **year**.

Word _____
        year

Translation _____

Make Connections _____

_____

month

month
(noun)

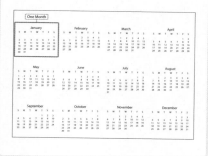

There are 12 **months** in a year. The first **month** is January.

Word _____
       month

Translation _____

Make Connections _____

_____

today

to • **day**
(noun)

We have soccer practice **today**.

Word _____
       today

Translation _____

Make Connections _____

_____

yesterday

yes • ter • **day**
(noun)

We had art club **yesterday**.

Word _____
       yesterday

Translation _____

Make Connections _____

_____

tomorrow

to • **mor** • row
(noun)

Yesterday | Today | Tomorrow

We have music club **tomorrow**.

Word _____
tomorrow

Translation _____

Make Connections _____

_____

birthday

birth • day
(noun)

My **birthday** is the day I was born.

Word _____
birthday

Translation _____

Make Connections _____

_____

start

start
(verb)

October 1, 2022
10/1/2022

The month **starts** on October 1st.

Word _____
start

Translation _____

Make Connections _____

_____

Vocabulary Review

calendar	month	yesterday	birthday
year	today	tomorrow	start

Share translations with a partner.

LANGUAGE TO SHARE TRANSLATIONS 💬

What language do you speak?

I speak (language).

Can you share a word in (language)?

The (language) word for _____ is _____.

Practice saying months and years. Then answer the question.

Months in a Year
1. January
2. February
3. March
4. April
5. May
6. June
7. July
8. August
9. September
10. October
11. November
12. December

Year	Say It
2000	two thousand
...	
2010	two thousand ten
...	
2020	two thousand twenty
2021	two thousand twenty-one
2022	two thousand twenty-two
2023	two thousand twenty-three
2024	two thousand twenty-four

What is **today's** date?

Today is _____.

(Month day, year)

Language Builder

Telling the Date

Ordinal numbers tell the order of things.

*January is the **first** month of the year.*

Use ordinal numbers to say the **day**.

*My birthday is May **1st**.*

Number	Ordinal Number	
1	first	1st
2	second	2nd
3	third	3rd
4	fourth	4th
5	fifth	5th

To say a date in the United States, say the **month**, **day**, and **year**. When you write the date, add a comma after the day.

March 25th, 2027

You can also write the date using numbers, like this:

month/day/year

3/25/2027

Use **on** or **in** to tell <u>when</u> something happens.

on a specific date or day	*School starts **on** <u>August 28th</u>.* *School starts **on** <u>Thursday</u>.*
in a month or year	*I was born **in** <u>December</u>.* *I was born **in** <u>2010</u>.*

Highlight the month, year, or date. <u>Underline</u> *on* or *in*.

Model: Vincent was born <u>in</u> June.

1. Genevieve was born in 2008.

2. Julia was born on April 13th, 2011.

3. Silas starts dance class on September 29th.

4. Hazel starts classes at a new school

   in February.

> **LANGUAGE TO SHARE IDEAS** 💬
>
> What did you highlight?
>
> I highlighted _____.
>
> ....
>
> What did you underline?
>
> I underlined _____.

Write *on* or *in* before the month, year, or date.

Model: Vincent was born ___on___ June 2nd.
        (in/on)

1. Sergio was born _____ May 8th, 2009.
        (in/on)

2. Patricia starts basketball _____ November.
            (in/on)

3. Diana has science class _____ Tuesday.
            (in/on)

4. Dante was born _____ 2007.
        (in/on)

> **LANGUAGE TO SHARE IDEAS** 💬
>
> What did you write?
>
> I wrote _____.

Listen Up

Listen to the conversation.

 Hi, Taikhira! When were you born?

I was born on March 21st.

When did you start classes at Lancaster Academy?

I started classes in May.

Talk About It

Partner A, **ask questions.** Partner B, **respond. Then switch roles.**

A: Hi, _____!
       (Name)

When were you born?

B: I was born on _____.
            (Month day, year)

A: When did you start classes at _____
                          (School Name)

_____?

B: I started classes in _____.
           (Month)

WORD BANK

Months

January	May	September
February	June	October
March	July	November
April	August	December

Functional Text: Calendar

A **calendar** helps you organize your **schedule**.

Calendars show the **year**, **month**, and **day of the week**.

Each day has a number, or **date**.

Write **events** or important dates on your calendar so you remember them.

October

Sunday	Monday	Tuesday	Wednesday	Thursday	Friday	Saturday
						1
2	3	4 Math Test	5 Computer Club	6	7 Basketball Game at 5:00 p.m.	8
9	10	11	12 Computer Club	13	14	15 Thao's Birthday Party at 11:00 a.m.
16	17	18	19 Computer Club	20	21 Basketball Game at 5:00 p.m.	22
23	24 Science Test	25	26 Computer Club	27	28 Math Test	29
30 Movies with Alex at 3:00 p.m.	31					

Read and Respond

Read the calendar to answer the questions.

1. When is the birthday party?

- (a) Saturday, October 15th

- (b) Saturday, October 22nd

- (c) Wednesday, October 26th

2. When is the science test?

- (a) Saturday, October 15th

- (b) Monday, October 24th

- (c) Wednesday, October 26th

3. How many math tests are in October?

- (a) one

- (b) two

- (c) three

4. What day of the week is Computer Club?

- (a) Monday

- (b) Wednesday

- (c) Friday

Write About It

Write sentences about the dates for today, yesterday, and tomorrow.

Model: What is today's date?

Today is _____.
        (Month day, year)

1. What was yesterday's date?

Yesterday was _____.
             (Month day, year)

2. What is tomorrow's date?

Tomorrow is _____.
           (Month day, year)

LANGUAGE TO COLLABORATE 💬

What can we write?

We can write _____.

WORD BANK 🧩

Months

January	July
February	August
March	September
April	October
May	November
June	December

Don't Forget!

Use **on** or **in** to tell <u>when</u> something happens.

*School starts **on** <u>August 28</u>.*

*We have seven basketball games **in** <u>December</u>.*

Write sentences about events at your school.

Model: The drama performance is on _____.
(Month day, year)

1. My first day of school was on _____.
(Month day, year)

2. _____ is _____ _____.
(Event) *(in/on)* *(Month day)*

3. _____ is _____ _____.
(Event) *(in/on)* *(Month)*

4. _____ is _____ _____.
(Event) *(in/on)* *(year)*

LANGUAGE TO SHARE IDEAS

What did you write?

I wrote _____.

Well done! Now you can talk about when things happen at home or at school. Tell your partner an important date, like your birthday or an event at school: *(Event) is on (Month day, year)*.

Weather Report

What's the weather today? Is it going to be hot or cold? Let's learn how to describe the weather.

✦ Vocabulary Builder

1. Say It   **2.** See It   **3.** Read It   **4.** Write It

weather

weath • er
(noun)

The **weather** is what it is like outside today.

Word _____
  weather

Translation _____

Make Connections _____

_____

sunny

sun • ny
(adjective)

We like being outside when the sun is out and it is **sunny**.

Word _____
  sunny

Translation _____

Make Connections _____

_____

rainy
rain • y
(adjective)

When it is a **rainy** day, I bring my umbrella.

Word _____
         rainy

Translation _____

Make Connections _____

_____

cloudy
cloud • y
(adjective)

There are lots of clouds in the sky on a **cloudy** day.

Word _____
         cloudy

Translation _____

Make Connections _____

_____

windy
wind • y
(adjective)

When it is **windy**, the air blows around me.

Word _____
         windy

Translation _____

Make Connections _____

_____

Vocabulary and Language

temperature

tem • per • a • **ture**
(noun)

The **temperature** is how hot or cold it is outside.

Word _____
            temperature

Translation _____

Make Connections _____

_____

cold

cold
(adjective)

The temperature is low, and it is **cold** outside.

Word _____
            cold

Translation _____

Make Connections _____

_____

hot

hot
(adjective)

The temperature is high, and it is **hot** outside.

Word _____
            hot

Translation _____

Make Connections _____

_____

Vocabulary Review

weather	rainy	windy	cold
sunny	cloudy	temperature	hot

Share translations with a partner.

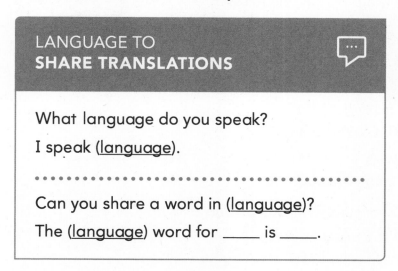

LANGUAGE TO
SHARE TRANSLATIONS

What language do you speak?

I speak (language).

....

Can you share a word in (language)?

The (language) word for _____ is _____.

What are other words you can use to describe the weather?

These are other words you can use to describe the **weather**:

- _____

- _____

- _____

- _____

- _____

 **Language Builder**

Contractions

A **contraction** is two words put together to form one shorter word.

An **apostrophe** takes the place of the missing letter or letters.

> ***What is*** *the weather today?*
> → ***What's*** *the weather today?*
> ***It is*** *rainy today.*
> → ***It's*** *rainy today.*
> ***I am*** *using an umbrella.*
> → ***I'm*** *using an umbrella.*

Many contractions are formed with a **pronoun** or with a **question word** and the **verb *to be***.

Pronouns	Question Words
I am = I'm	what is = what's
you are = you're	who is = who's
he is = he's	how is = how's
she is = she's	
it is = it's	
we are = we're	
they are = they're	

Write a contraction to complete each sentence.

Model: _____I'm_____ cold and need to go inside.
    _(I am)_

1. _____ happy to be outside when it is sunny.
   _(He is)_

2. _____ often 95 degrees and sunny in July.
   _(It is)_

3. _____ going to bring an umbrella today!
   (They are)

4. _____ always happy when the temperature is warm.
   (She is)

5. _____ waiting for the rain to stop.
   (We are)

6. _____ going to check the temperature.
   (You are)

LANGUAGE TO SHARE IDEAS 💬

What did you write?

I wrote _____.

Listen Up

Listen to the conversation.

 Hi, Taikhira! How's the weather today?

Today is warm. The temperature is 75 degrees.

Is it rainy or sunny?

It's sunny right now.

Talk About It

Partner A, **ask questions.** Partner B, **respond. Then switch roles.**

A: Hi, _____!
    (Name)
    What's the weather today?

B: Today the weather is _____. The temperature is
                            (adjective)
    _____ degrees.
    (number)

A: Is it rainy or sunny?

B: It's _____ right now. It's also _____.
            (adjective)   (adjective)

WORD BANK		🧩
Adjectives (describing words)		
cloudy	hot	sunny
cold	rainy	warm
cool	snowy	windy

Listen and Respond

Listen to the weather report.

Take notes on the weather report.

Topic: Weather Report

Today's weather: _____ and _____
  (cold/hot) (sunny/windy)

Today's temperature: _____ degrees
  (25/75)

Tomorrow's weather: _____
  (colder and rainy/warmer and sunny)

_____

Answer the questions.

1. Which activity could you do with your friends today in Denver?

   (a) ride your bikes in a park

   (b) cook your favorite meal

   (c) play soccer at an outdoor field

2. Why does Arlo say that it is "good news" that the weather will be "sunny and 35 degrees" tomorrow?

   (a) It is good news because the temperature will be colder.

   (b) It is good news because the temperature will be warmer.

   (c) It is good news because Arlo will have to give another weather report.

Write About It

>  **Remember!**
>
> A **contraction** is two words put together with an apostrophe.
>
> *It is* sunny today. → *It's* sunny today.
>
> *We are* sitting outside. → *We're* sitting outside.

Write a weather report with your teacher.

Model: Hello, I'm Cameron Ruiz reporting from Franklin Middle School. It's November 12th, and it's rainy today! Right now, the temperature is 52 degrees. It's a good idea to hang out inside today. Thanks for listening to this weather report!

Hello, _____ _____ reporting
         (contraction: I + am)   (Name)

from _____.
         (School Name)

_____ _____, and _____
(contraction: It + is)   (date)   (contraction: it + is)

_____ today!
(adjective)

Right now, the temperature is _____ degrees. _____ a
                                    (number)   (contraction: It + is)

good idea to hang out _____ today.
                          (inside/outside)

Thanks for listening to this weather report!

What is your favorite type of weather? Write a weather report for your perfect day.

Hello, _____ _____ reporting
       (contraction: I + am)   *(Name)*

from _____.
    (School Name)

_____ _____,
(contraction: It + is)   *(date)*

and _____ _____ today!
   (contraction: it + is)   *(adjective)*

Right now, the temperature is _____ degrees. _____
                       (number)   *(contraction: It + is)*

a good idea to hang out _____ today.
                  (inside/outside)

Thanks for listening to this weather report!

WORD BANK

Adjectives (describing words)

cloudy	hot	sunny
cold	rainy	warm
cool	snowy	windy

LANGUAGE TO COLLABORATE

What can we write?

We can write _____.

Woo-hoo! Now you can talk about the weather.
Tell your partner what the weather is like today:
Today, it's (weather).

Common Ground

When we meet new friends, it's important to get to know them and learn what activities they like to do. Then you can discuss activities that you both enjoy—that's your common ground!

 ## Vocabulary Builder

1. Say It   **2.** See It   **3.** Read It   **4.** Write It

code

code
(verb)

I learned to **code** a new game for my computer.

Word _____
     code

Translation _____

Make Connections _____

_____

cook

cook
(verb)

I **cook** dinner in the kitchen with my dad.

Word _____
     cook

Translation _____

Make Connections _____

_____

create

cre • **ate**
(verb)

Joao **creates** his own bowls in pottery class.

Word _____
   create

Translation _____

Make Connections _____

_____

dance

dance
(verb)

The students **dance** during dance club after school.

Word _____
   dance

Translation _____

Make Connections _____

_____

draw

draw
(verb)

She likes to **draw** pictures of her friends.

Word _____
   draw

Translation _____

Make Connections _____

_____

ride

ride
(verb)

He **rides** his bicycle to school every day.

Word _____
       ride

Translation _____

Make Connections _____

_____

sing

sing
(verb)

The students **sing** at the school concert.

Word _____
       sing

Translation _____

Make Connections _____

_____

watch

watch
(verb)

Simon and his friends **watch** funny videos.

Word _____
       watch

Translation _____

Make Connections _____

_____

Vocabulary Review

| code | create | draw | sing |
| cook | dance | ride | watch |

Share translations with a partner.

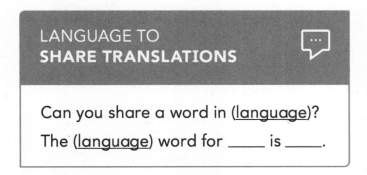

LANGUAGE TO
SHARE TRANSLATIONS

Can you share a word in (language)?

The (language) word for _____ is _____.

What are other activities you like to do?

These are other activities I like to do:

- _____
- _____
- _____
- _____
- _____

Language Builder

Yes/No Questions with the Verb *do*

Ask and answer yes/no questions with **do** or **does**.

- For *I*, *you*, *we*, and *they*, use **do** and **do not**.
- For *he* and *she*, use **does** and **does not**.

Question	Answers	
Do *you like to draw?*	Yes, I like to draw.	No, I **do not** like to draw.
Do *you like to draw?*	Yes, we like to draw.	No, we **do not** like to draw.
Do *they like to draw?*	Yes, they like to draw.	No, they **do not** like to draw.
Does *she like to draw?*	Yes, she likes to draw.	No, she **does not** like to draw.
Does *he like to draw?*	Yes, he likes to draw.	No, he **does not** like to draw.

To ask or answer a yes/no question about **two people**, use the word **both**.

*Do you **both** like to play soccer?*

*Yes, we **both** like to play soccer.*

Rewrite each sentence as a yes/no question with *do* or *does*.

Model: You like to play video games.

Do you like to play video games?

1. They like to bake bread.

_____

2. She likes to draw pictures.

_____

Answer the yes/no questions.

Model: Do you like to play video games?

Yes, I like to play video games.

1. Do they like to sing?

No, _____.

2. Does she like to listen to music?

Yes, _____.

3. Do you both like to dance?

Yes, _____.

LANGUAGE TO SHARE IDEAS

What did you write?

I wrote _____.

Listen Up

Listen to the conversation.

 Hi, Mateo! Do you like to cook food?

Hello, Serene! Yes, I like to cook food.

Cool! Do you like to play sports?

Yes, I like to play baseball. It's my favorite!

Talk About It

Partner A, **ask questions.** Partner B, **respond. Then switch roles.**

A: Hi, _____!
       (Name)

Do you like to _____?
              (verb phrase)

B: Hello, _____!
          (Name)

_____, I _____ to _____.
 (Yes/No)   (like/do not like)   (verb phrase)

A: Interesting! Do you like to _____?
                             (verb phrase)

B: _____, I _____ to _____.
    (Yes/No)   (like/do not like)   (verb phrase)

WORD BANK   ❖

Verb Phrases (action phrases)

code new programs   draw pictures   read books

create art   play sports   watch videos

dance to music   play video games   _____

Take notes on your partners' responses.

Classmate's Name	Interests

Reading a Venn Diagram

A **Venn diagram** shows the similarities and differences between two people, places, things, or ideas.

- Similarities are the ways that two things are the same.

- Differences are the ways that two things are different.

To read a Venn diagram:

1. Read the title to identify the topic.

2. Read the headings to identify who or what is being compared.

3. Read the left and right sections to find differences between the two people, places, things, or ideas being compared.

4. Read the middle section, where the shapes overlap, to find similarities.

Favorite Interests

Riad
- Play guitar
- Read books
- Visit family

Both
- Bake cookies
- Read graphic novels

Carmen
- Watch movies
- Play soccer
- Study math

Read and Respond

Read the Venn diagram to answer the questions.

1. What does Riad like to do?
   Riad likes to _____.

   (a) play soccer

   (b) read books

   (c) study math

2. What does Carmen like to do?
   Carmen likes to _____.

   (a) play guitar

   (b) read books

   (c) watch movies

3. What do Riad and Carmen both like to do?
   Riad and Carmen both like to _____.

   (a) play guitar

   (b) study math

   (c) bake cookies

4. Do both students like to play soccer?

   (a) Yes, both students like to play soccer.

   (b) No, only one student likes to play soccer.

Create a Venn Diagram

List three activities you like to do.

I like to . . .

- _____

- _____

- _____

Discuss activities with your partner. Take notes on activities you both like and activities that only your partner likes.

A: I like to _____.
        (verb phrase)

    Do you like to _____?
                (verb phrase)

B: Yes, I like to _____.
                (verb phrase)

    OR

B: No, I do not like to _____.
                    (verb phrase)

Take notes.

I like to . . .	We both like to . . .	My partner likes to . . .

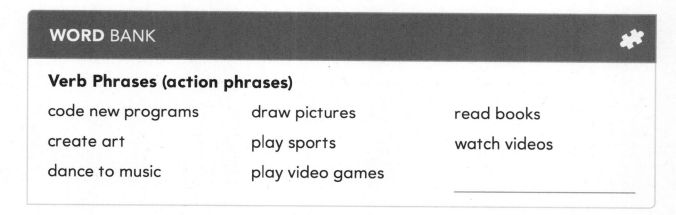

WORD BANK

Verb Phrases (action phrases)

code new programs · draw pictures · read books

create art · play sports · watch videos

dance to music · play video games · _____

Complete the Venn diagram with similarities and differences between you and your partner.

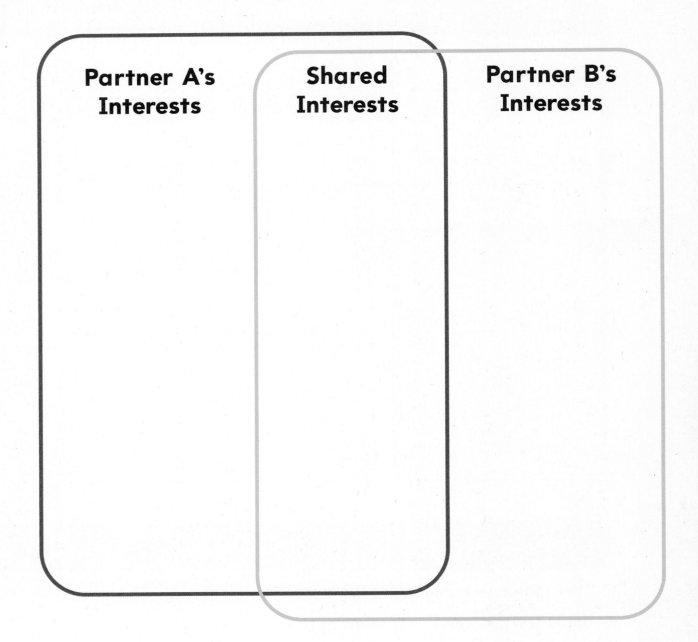

Partner A's Interests   **Shared Interests**   **Partner B's Interests**

Write About It

Write sentences about your Venn diagram.

1. I like to _____.
   (verb phrase)

2. My partner likes to _____.
   (verb phrase)

3. We both like to _____.
   (verb phrase)

4. We both also like to _____.
   (verb phrase)

LANGUAGE TO SHARE IDEAS 💬

What did you write?

I wrote _____.

Bravo! Now you can find common interests between you and your friends. Share your favorite activity with a partner and find out if they like it too: *I like to (verb phrase). Do you like to (verb phrase)?*

What to Wear

I might wear different clothes when it's hot or cold or when I'm going to a specific event. Let's talk about what to wear!

 ## Vocabulary Builder

1. Say It   **2.** See It   **3.** Read It   **4.** Write It

---

wear

wear
(verb)

Jonah is choosing what to **wear** to school.

Word _____
      wear

Translation _____

Make Connections _____

_____

---

color

col • or
(noun)

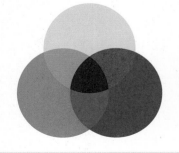

Clothes come in so many different **colors**!

Word _____
      color

Translation _____

Make Connections _____

_____

shirt

shirt
(noun)

Luna's **shirt** is black.

Word _____
       shirt

Translation _____

Make Connections _____

_____

pants

pants
(noun)

She is wearing gray **pants**.

Word _____
       pants

Translation _____

Make Connections _____

_____

dress

dress
(noun)

Jira is wearing a yellow **dress**.

Word _____
       dress

Translation _____

Make Connections _____

_____

jacket

jack • et
(noun)

Benji has a green **jacket**.

Word _____
     jacket

Translation _____

Make Connections _____

_____

shoes

shoes
(noun)

Sam wears **shoes** for running.

Word _____
     shoes

Translation _____

Make Connections _____

_____

glasses

glass • es
(noun)

Philip's black **glasses** help him see clearly!

Word _____
     glasses

Translation _____

Make Connections _____

_____

Vocabulary Review

wear	shirt	dress	shoes
color	pants	jacket	glasses

Share translations with a partner.

LANGUAGE TO SHARE TRANSLATIONS 💬

Can you share a word in (language)?

The (language) word for _____ is _____.

THINGS YOU CAN WEAR	
Type	**Examples**
Tops	button-down shirt, sweater, t-shirt
Bottoms	jeans, shorts, skirt
Shoes	boots, sandals, sneakers
Outerwear	coat, sweatshirt, windbreaker
Accessories	gloves, scarf, sunglasses
Other	pajamas, uniform

What are things you wear?

These are things I **wear**:

- _____

- _____

- _____

Language Builder

Adjectives

An **adjective** is a word that describes a noun—a person, place, thing, or idea.

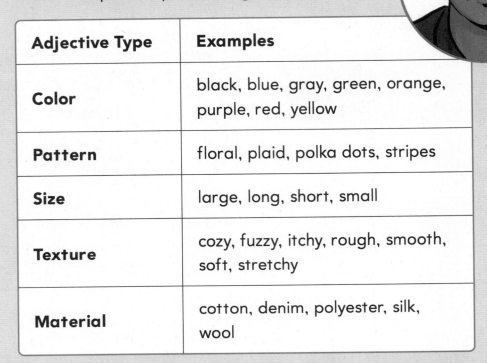

Adjective Type	Examples
Color	black, blue, gray, green, orange, purple, red, yellow
Pattern	floral, plaid, polka dots, stripes
Size	large, long, short, small
Texture	cozy, fuzzy, itchy, rough, smooth, soft, stretchy
Material	cotton, denim, polyester, silk, wool

An adjective often comes **before** the <u>noun</u> that it describes.

*I have a **blue** <u>shirt</u>.*
*I have a **cozy** <u>sweatshirt</u>.*

WORD BANK

Nouns (things)

coat	glasses	jacket	shirt
dress	hat	pants	shoes

Look at each image and complete the sentence.

Model: My friend has a ___blue___ ___hat___.
                       (adjective) *(noun)*

> **LANGUAGE TO SHARE IDEAS**
>
> What did you write?
>
> I wrote _____.

1. Jira has a _____
         (adjective)

_____.
(noun)

2. Joey has a _____
         (adjective)

_____.
(noun)

3. Philip has _____
         (adjective)

_____.
(noun)

4. My friend has a _____
         (adjective)

_____.
(noun)

 **Listen Up**

Listen to the conversation.

▶ Hi, Shaun! What will you wear to the talent show?

I will wear a black shirt and black pants.

What will you wear to the soccer game?

I will wear a blue soccer jersey and red sneakers.

Talk About It

Partner A, **ask questions.** Partner B, **respond. Then switch roles.**

A: Hi! What will you wear to the _____ ?
(event)

B: I will wear my _____ _____
(adjective) (noun)

and my _____ _____ .
(adjective) (noun)

A: What will you wear to the _____ ?
(event)

B: I will wear my _____ _____
(adjective) (noun)

and my _____ _____ .
(adjective) (noun)

WORD BANK

Adjectives (describing words)

black	orange
blue	purple
brown	red
green	yellow

Nouns (things)

dress	sneakers
pants	sweatshirt
shirt	uniform

_____

Make Observations

Look at the pictures. Discuss what you see. Take notes to help you.

1. _____
_____
_____
_____

2. _____
_____
_____
_____

3. _____
_____
_____
_____

4. _____
_____
_____
_____

5. _____

_____

_____

_____

6. _____

_____

_____

_____

WORD BANK

Adjectives (describing words)			Nouns (things)			
blue	orange	red	coat	jeans	shirt	sunglasses
brown	pink	yellow	hat	pajamas	socks	vest
green	purple	white	jacket	pants	sweater	uniform

LANGUAGE TO OBSERVE

What do you see?

I see _____ wearing a _____.

What else do you see?

I also see _____ wearing a _____.

Read and Respond

Read the text. Then answer the questions.

1   The weather affects what you **wear**. Is it a hot, sunny day?
A short-sleeved **shirt** can help you beat the heat. And don't forget
your sunglasses! But on a cool day, you might reach for a hat and
a cozy sweater. On cold snowy days, you might also **wear** a **jacket**
and gloves to stay warm.

2   Your plans also affect what you choose to **wear**. Are you
playing a baseball game? Then you might need to wear a baseball
uniform. But if you're going to a family event, a nice **shirt** and
pants or a **dress** would be the better choice. And what's perfect
for when you're staying home? Pajamas!

1. What might you think about when choosing clothes to wear?

   I might think about the _____
   (noun)

   or my _____.
   (noun)

2. What does it mean to "beat the heat"?

   (a) get hot

   (b) stay cool

   (c) reach for a hat

3. For a family event, a nice shirt is a better choice than ____.

   (a) a dress

   (b) nice pants

   (c) a baseball uniform

4. When are pajamas the perfect choice?

   (a) at home

   (b) at a family event

   (c) at a baseball game

Write About It

 Remember!

An **adjective** is a word that describes a <u>noun</u>.

*I love to wear my **green** <u>shirt</u>.*

An adjective often comes before the noun it describes.

Imagine you are going to a special event. What is the event, and what would you wear?

Model: If I were going to <u>my best friend's birthday party</u>, I would wear my <u>orange</u> <u>jacket</u>. I would also wear my <u>white</u> <u>shirt</u> and <u>blue</u> <u>jeans</u>.

If I were going to _____,
(special event)

I would wear my _____
(adjective)

_____.
(noun)

I would also wear my _____
(adjective)

_____
(noun)

and _____
(adjective)

_____.
(noun)

WORD BANK

Adjectives (describing words)

black	nice
blue	orange
brown	pink
favorite	purple
green	red
new	yellow

Nouns (things)

dress	shirt
hat	shoes
jacket	sneakers
pants	uniform

_____

Fantastic! Now you can describe what you are wearing. Tell your partner what you think you might wear on a cold day: *On a cold day, I might wear (a/an)* _(adjective)_ _(noun)_.

Everyday Habits

Some people play soccer every day. Some people read every afternoon. What are some of your habits? Let's learn about some of the things people do every day.

 ## Vocabulary Builder

1. Say It   **2.** See It   **3.** Read It   **4.** Write It

wake up

wake up
(verb)

I **wake up** at 7:15 a.m. every day.

Word _____
     wake up
Translation _____

Make Connections _____

_____

wash

wash
(verb)

I **wash** my face in the morning.

Word _____
     wash
Translation _____

Make Connections _____

_____

brush my teeth

brush my teeth
(verb phrase)

I **brush my teeth** with toothpaste and a toothbrush.

Word _____
   brush my teeth

Translation _____

Make Connections _____

_____

check

check
(verb)

I **check** my schedule to see my plans for the day.

Word _____
   check

Translation _____

Make Connections _____

_____

leave

leave
(verb)

I **leave** for school at 8:30 a.m.

Word _____
   leave

Translation _____

Make Connections _____

_____

Vocabulary and Language

exercise

ex • er • **cise**
(verb)

I **exercise** by going for a run.

Word _____
       exercise

Translation _____

Make Connections _____

_____

take a shower

take a **show** • er
(verb phrase)

I **take a shower** at night.

Word _____
      take a shower

Translation _____

Make Connections _____

_____

go to sleep

go to sleep
(verb phrase)

I **go to sleep** at 10:30 p.m.

Word _____
      go to sleep

Translation _____

Make Connections _____

_____

Vocabulary Review

wake up	brush my teeth	leave	take a shower
wash	check	exercise	go to sleep

Share translations with a partner.

> **LANGUAGE TO SHARE TRANSLATIONS**
>
> Can you share a word in (language)?
> The (language) word for _____ is _____.

What are other habits, or things you do every day?

These are other habits, or things I do every day:

- _____
- _____
- _____
- _____
- _____

Language Builder

Adverbs to Tell How Often

An **adverb** describes an action. Some adverbs tell <u>how often</u> an action happens.

Adverb	Purpose	Examples
always	Use for something you do <u>every day</u>.	I **always** wake up at 7:15 a.m.
often usually	Use for something you do <u>most days</u>.	I **often** exercise before school. I **usually** exercise before school.
sometimes	Use for something you do <u>some days</u>.	I **sometimes** eat a snack after school.
never	Use for something you <u>do not do</u>.	I **never** go to sleep before 9 p.m.

Write the adverb under the image it matches.

Sunday	Monday	Tuesday	Wednesday	Thursday	Friday	Saturday
✓	✓	✓	✓	✓	✓	✓

_____

Sunday	Monday	Tuesday	Wednesday	Thursday	Friday	Saturday
	✓	✓		✓	✓	✓

_____

Sunday	Monday	Tuesday	Wednesday	Thursday	Friday	Saturday
	✓		✓		✓	

_____

Sunday	Monday	Tuesday	Wednesday	Thursday	Friday	Saturday

_____

always	never	sometimes	usually

Listen Up

Listen to the conversation.

 Hi, Taikhira! What time do you wake up?

Hello, Shaun! I usually wake up at 6:45 a.m.

Wow! What time do you leave for school?

I always leave for school at 7:30 a.m.

Talk About It

Remember! Write the time with numerals, but use the words **fifteen**, **thirty**, and **forty-five** when saying the time.

Write	Say
7:00 a.m.	seven a.m.
7:15 a.m.	seven **fifteen** a.m.
7:30 a.m.	seven **thirty** a.m.
7:45 a.m.	seven **forty-five** a.m.

Partner A, **ask questions.** Partner B, **respond. Then switch roles.**

A: Hi, _____!
   (Name)

   What time do you wake up?

B: Hello, _____!
   (Name)

   I _____ wake up at _____.
       (adverb)   (time)

A: Wow! What time do you leave for school?

B: I _____ leave for school at _____.
      (adverb)   (time)

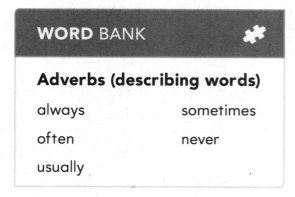

WORD BANK

Adverbs (describing words)

always	sometimes
often	never
usually	

Make Observations

Look at the pictures. Discuss what you see. Take notes to help you.

1. _____

_____

_____

2. _____

_____

_____

_____

3. _____

_____

_____

4. _____

_____

_____

5. _____

_____

_____

6. _____

_____

_____

7. _____

_____

_____

8. _____

_____

_____

WORD BANK

Verb Phrases (action phrases)

wake up	brush teeth	leave for school	take a shower
wash face	check schedule	exercise	go to sleep

LANGUAGE TO OBSERVE

What do you see?   :   What else do you see?

I see ____.   :   I also see ____.

Read and Respond

Read the text. Then answer the questions.

Tam wakes up.

She washes her face.

She brushes her teeth.

She checks her schedule.

She leaves for school.

She exercises.

She takes a shower.

She goes to sleep.

What's a typical day for Tam? She usually **wakes up** at 7:15 a.m. After **waking up**, she **washes** her face. She never forgets to **brush her teeth**. Next, she **checks** her schedule. She always **leaves** for school at 8:30 a.m. When she gets home from school, she sometimes **exercises**. Tam often **takes a shower** before she **goes to sleep**. She's always in bed by 10:45 p.m. What's a typical day for you?

1. What does Tam usually do at 7:15 a.m.?

   Tam usually _____ at 7:15 a.m.
                  (verb phrase)

2. What does Tam always do at 8:30 a.m.?

   At 8:30 a.m., Tam always _____.
                      (verb phrase)

3. What does Tam do sometimes after school?

   Tam _____ _____ after school.
       (adverb)   *(verb phrase)*

4. When does Tam go to sleep?

   Tam _____ goes to sleep by _____.
       (adverb)   *(time)*

5. What does Tam never forget?

   Tam _____.

WORD BANK

Verb Phrases (action phrases)		**Adverbs (describing words)**	
brushes her teeth	leaves for school	always	sometimes
checks her schedule	takes a shower	often	never
exercises	wakes up	usually	
goes to sleep	washes her face		

Write About It

 Don't Forget!

Use **adverbs** to tell <u>how often</u> you do something.

- Use **always** to tell about something you do <u>every day</u>.

- Use **often** or **usually** to tell about something you do <u>most days</u>.

- Use **sometimes** to tell about something you do <u>some days</u>.

- Use **never** to tell about something you <u>do not do</u>.

Write sentences about your everyday habits.

Model: I always _____
(verb phrase)

_____ I _____.
(before/after) *(verb phrase)*

1. I _____ wake up at _____.
(adverb) *(time)*

2. I usually _____ _____
(verb phrase) *(before/after)*

I _____.
(verb phrase)

3. I _____ go to sleep at _____.
(adverb) *(time)*

4. I sometimes _____ _____
(verb phrase) *(before/after)*

I _____.
(verb phrase)

5. I never _____.
(verb phrase)

Write a paragraph about your everyday habits.

Model: I do many things during the day. I always wake up at 7:00 a.m.
I usually exercise before I leave for school. I often leave for school at 8:15 a.m.
I sometimes exercise before I go to sleep. I never go to sleep before 10:00 p.m.

_____

_____

_____

_____

_____

_____

WORD BANK

Verb Phrases (action phrases)		**Adverbs (describing words)**	
brush my teeth	take a shower	always	sometimes
exercise	wake up	often	never
go to sleep	wash my face	usually	
leave for school	_____		

Wonderful! Now you can talk about your habits. Tell your
partner two of your habits: _I always (habit). I often (habit)._

A Day in My Life

There are so many things I do in a day!
Let's talk about a day in my life.

 ## Vocabulary Builder

1. Say It   **2.** See It   **3.** Read It   **4.** Write It

active

ac • tive
(adjective)

Kholoud is **active** when she exercises in the morning.

Word _____
          active

Translation _____

Make Connections _____

_____

creative

cre • a • tive
(adjective)

I am **creative** when I paint or draw.

Word _____
          creative

Translation _____

Make Connections _____

_____

helpful

help • ful
(adjective)

Sun is **helpful** when he washes the dishes.

Word _____
helpful

Translation _____

Make Connections _____

_____

homework

home • work
(noun)

John does his **homework** after school every day.

Word _____
homework

Translation _____

Make Connections _____

_____

musical

mu • si • cal
(adjective)

I am **musical** because I play the guitar.

Word _____
musical

Translation _____

Make Connections _____

_____

Vocabulary and Language

social

so • cial
(adjective)

Frankie likes being **social** and hanging out with his friends.

Word _____
  social

Translation _____

Make Connections _____

_____

work

work
(verb)

I **work** at the grocery store from 5:00 p.m. to 8:00 p.m.

Word _____
  work

Translation _____

Make Connections _____

_____

spend time

spend time
(verb phrase)

I **spend time** doing many things outside.

Word _____
  spend time

Translation _____

Make Connections _____

_____

 **Vocabulary Review**

| active | helpful | musical | work |
| creative | homework | social | spend time |

Share translations with a partner.

LANGUAGE TO SHARE TRANSLATIONS

Can you share a word in (language)?
The (language) word for _____ is _____.

Complete each sentence.

1. I like to **spend time** being _____. For example,
   (adjective)

   I _____.
   (verb phrase)

2. I also like to **spend time** being _____. For example,
   (adjective)

   I _____.
   (verb phrase)

Language Builder

> **Prepositions:** *from*, *to*
>
> Use **from** and **to** to tell how much time you spend doing an activity.
>
> Use **from** to tell when an activity starts. Use **to** to tell when an activity ends.
>
> > I read **from** 9:00 p.m. **to** 10:00 p.m.
> > I spend one hour reading.
>
> > I have practice **from** 3:00 p.m. **to** 5:00 p.m.
> > I spend two hours at practice.

Highlight the activity. **Underline** the prepositions that tell when the activity starts and ends.

Model: She spends time watching videos from 4:00 p.m. to 5:00 p.m.

1. Jermaine spends time being active from 3:00 p.m. to 4:00 p.m.

2. I am usually more social from 7:00 p.m. to 10:00 p.m.

3. Soledad spends time texting with friends from 5 p.m. to 6 p.m.

4. Luis usually sleeps from 10:00 p.m. to 6:00 a.m.

5. Abigail goes for a run from 3:30 p.m. to 4:00 p.m.

LANGUAGE TO SHARE IDEAS 💬
What did you highlight?
I highlighted _____.
··························
What did you underline?
I underlined _____.

Complete the sentences.

Model: I spend time watching videos _____from_____ 6:00 p.m. _____to_____ 8:00 p.m.
(preposition)   (preposition)

I spend _____two_____ hours watching television.
(number)

1. I hang out with my friends _____ 2:30 p.m. _____ 3:30 p.m.
(preposition)   (preposition)

I spend one hour hanging out with friends.

2. I usually practice soccer _____ 3:30 p.m. _____ 4:30 p.m.
(preposition)   (preposition)

I spend _____ hour practicing soccer.
(number)

3. I do homework _____ 7:30 p.m. _____ _____
(preposition)   (preposition)   (time)

I spend _____ doing homework.
(number of hours or minutes)

LANGUAGE TO SHARE IDEAS 💬

What did you write?

I wrote _____.

Speaking and Listening

 Listen Up

Listen to the conversation.

▶ Hi, Mateo! How do you spend your free time?

Oh, hello, Serene! I spend my free time being active.

That's great! What do you do?

I usually play basketball from 4:00 p.m. to 6:00 p.m., so I spend two hours being active.

Talk About It

Partner A, ask questions. Partner B, respond. Then switch roles.

A: Hi, _____!
(Name)

How do you spend your free time?

B: Hello, _____.
(Name)

I spend my free time being _____.
(adjective)

A: That's great! What do you do?

B: I _____ from _____ to _____.
(verb phrase) _(time)_ _(time)_

I spend _____ hour(s) being _____.
(number) _(adjective)_

WORD BANK ✦

Adjectives (describing words)

active	helpful	social
creative	musical	_____

Listen and take notes on your classmates' responses.

Name	Activity	Time

Reading a Pie Chart

A **pie chart** shows information in a circular graph. A pie chart is divided into pieces or slices. Each piece represents a number or percentage. The entire circle or pie is equal to the total number or 100 percent (100%).

To read a pie chart:

1. Place your finger on the biggest piece of the pie chart.

2. Identify the category for that piece and the amount it represents.

3. Move your finger to the next piece and repeat the process.

A Day in My Life

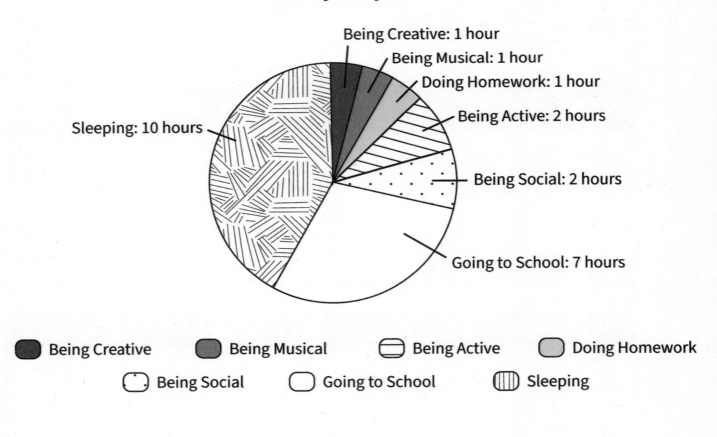

Being Creative: 1 hour
Being Musical: 1 hour
Doing Homework: 1 hour
Being Active: 2 hours
Being Social: 2 hours
Sleeping: 10 hours
Going to School: 7 hours

Being Creative   Being Musical   Being Active   Doing Homework

Being Social   Going to School   Sleeping

Read and Respond

Read the pie chart to answer the questions.

1. What does the pie chart show?

    (a) a 7-hour day in a student's life

    (b) a 10-hour day in a student's life

    (c) a 24-hour day in a student's life

2. How many hours does the student spend being social?
    The student spends _____ hours being social.

    (a) 2

    (b) 7

    (c) 10

3. What activity does the student spend the most time doing?
    The student spends the most time _____.

    (a) sleeping

    (b) being social

    (c) going to school

Writing

 Create a Pie Chart

How do you spend your time? Write the activities you do during the day. Then write how many hours you spend doing each activity.

Color	Activity	Number of Hours

WORD BANK

Verb + –ing Phrases (action phrases)

| being active | being musical | doing homework | sleeping |
| being creative | being social | going to school | working |

Write About It

Create a pie chart. Fill in the pieces of the pie with a different color for each activity. Each piece of pie is equal to one hour of time.

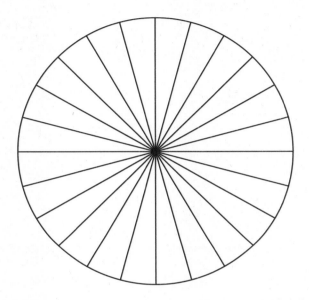

Write about your pie chart.

1. I spend the most time _____.

  (verb + –ing phrase)

2. I spend the least time _____.

  (verb + –ing phrase)

3. My favorite activity is _____.

  (verb + –ing phrase)

 I spend _____ hour(s) _____.

  (number)   *(verb + –ing phrase)*

Good job! Now you can talk about a day in your life. Tell your partner what your favorite weekend activity is: *My favorite weekend activity is (verb + –ing phrase).*

Catching Up

I have family and friends who live far away. I don't see them every day. So I send emails to tell them what is happening in my life! Let's learn how we can catch up with family and friends over email.

 ## Vocabulary Builder

1. Say It   **2.** See It   **3.** Read It   **4.** Write It

explore
ex • **plore**
(verb)

Let's **explore** the park and see what we can learn!

Word _____
　　　explore

Translation _____

Make Connections _____

_____

finish
fin • ish
(verb)

When I **finish** my chores, I am happy.

Word _____
　　　finish

Translation _____

Make Connections _____

_____

help

help
(verb)

I **help** my sister with her homework.

Word _____
     help

Translation _____

Make Connections _____

_____

join

join
(verb)

I **join** the debate team every year.

Word _____
     join

Translation _____

Make Connections _____

_____

make

make
(verb)

I like to **make** videos on my phone.

Word _____
     make

Translation _____

Make Connections _____

_____

tell

tell
(verb)

I like to **tell** my friend about my day.

Word _____
　　　　tell

Translation _____

Make Connections _____

_____

visit

vis • it
(verb)

I am excited to **visit** my grandparents.

Word _____
　　　　visit

Translation _____

Make Connections _____

_____

win

win
(verb)

Our team **wins** when we work together.

Word _____
　　　　win

Translation _____

Make Connections _____

_____

Vocabulary Review

explore	help	make	visit
finish	join	tell	win

Share translations with a partner.

> LANGUAGE TO
> **SHARE TRANSLATIONS**
>
> Can you share a word in (language)?
> The (language) word for _____ is _____.

Write sentences using new vocabulary.

1. I **explore** _____ to learn more about it.

2. When I **finish** my _____, I am happy.

3. I am excited to **visit** _____.

> LANGUAGE TO
> **SHARE IDEAS**
>
> What did you write?
> I wrote _____.

Language Builder

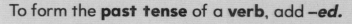

Past-Tense Verbs

A **verb** is an **action word**. A **past-tense verb** tells about an action that happened in the past.

*Yesterday, I **finished** a book.*

To form the **past tense** of a **verb**, add **–ed.**

finish → **finish<u>ed</u>**   help → **help<u>ed</u>**   join → **join<u>ed</u>**

If the **verb** ends in **–e**, add **–d.**

explore → **explore<u>d</u>**

Watch out! Some verbs are **irregular**. To form the **past tense**, you spell them in a new way. You need to remember these verbs.

am/is → **was**   go → **went**   tell → **told**

are → **were**   have → **had**   win → **won**

do → **did**   make → **made**

Write the past-tense of each regular verb.

Regular Verb	Past-Tense Verb
cook	
create	
explore	
finish	
help	
join	
visit	

LANGUAGE TO COLLABORATE

What can we write?

We can write _____.

Match each irregular verb to the past-tense form.

am	went
do	told
go	made
have	did
make	was
tell	had

LANGUAGE TO SHARE IDEAS

Which verbs did you match?

I matched the verbs _____ and _____.

Listen Up

Listen to the conversation.

> ▶ Hello, Taikhira! What did you do yesterday?

> Hi, Shaun! Yesterday, I joined the arts club.

> That's great! What else did you do yesterday?

> I also finished my science project.

Talk About It

Partner A, **ask questions.** Partner B, **respond. Then switch roles.**

A: Hello, _____!
           (Name)

    What did you do yesterday?

B: Hi, _____!
         (Name)

    Yesterday, I _____
              (past-tense verb)

_____.
(noun phrase)

A: That's great! What else did you do yesterday?

B: I also _____
          (past-tense verb)

_____.
(noun phrase)

WORD BANK

Verbs (action words)		**Noun Phrases (people, places, things)**	
explored	made	a book	a story
finished	told	a game	a video
helped	visited	a painting	my brother
joined	won	a park	the science club
_____		_____	

Functional Text: Email

An **email** is a message you send using the internet.

1. In the **To** field, write an email address.

2. In the **Subject** field, tell what the email is about.

3. **Write** the message under the subject line.

   - **Start** your email by writing "Hi" or "Hello" and the name of the person you are writing to.

   - **End** your email with a closing and your name.

4. Click **Send** to send the email.

To: camilo@email.com

Subject: Catching Up

Hi Camilo!

It's been a long time! How are you? I'm doing well. My neighborhood has a new park. I explored it for hours! When you visit, we will have a ton of fun there! And guess what? I'm an artist now. I joined the arts club at school. I have already made two huge paintings.

I miss you! Please write back and tell me how you are doing.

Take care,

Enríque

Read and Respond

Read the email and take notes. Then answer the questions.

To: _____

Subject: _____

From: _____

LANGUAGE TO SHARE IDEAS

What did you write?

I wrote _____.

1. Why did Enríque email Camilo?

   (a) to plan a visit

   (b) to learn about Camilo

   (c) to tell about events in his life

2. What is the first event Enríque tells about?

   (a) He explored a park.

   (b) He joined an arts club.

   (c) He made two huge paintings.

Write About It

> 💡 **Don't Forget!**
>
> To form the **past tense** of a regular verb, add **–ed**.
>
> _finish_ → **finish<u>ed</u>**
>
> If the **verb** ends in **–e**, then add **–d**.
>
> _explore_ → **explor<u>ed</u>**
>
> Some **verbs** are irregular. To form the **past tense**, you spell them in a new way.
>
> _tell_ → **told**

Plan an email for catching up with someone.

1. Who do you want to catch up with?

I want to catch up with _____.
    (Name)

2. List three things you want to tell them.

- I _____ _____.
    (past-tense verb)   _(noun)_

- I _____ _____.
    (past-tense verb)   _(noun)_

- I _____ _____.
    (past-tense verb)   _(noun)_

LANGUAGE TO SHARE IDEAS

What did you write?

I wrote _____.

Write an email for catching up with someone.

Subject: _____
        (Subject)

Hi _____!
  (Name)

It's been a long time! How are you? I'm doing well. Since we last talked,

I _____ _____.
  (past-tense verb)   *(noun)*

I also _____ _____,
       (past-tense verb)   *(noun)*

and I _____ _____.
      (past-tense verb)   *(noun)*

I miss you! Please write back and tell me how you are doing.

Take care,

_____
(Name)

WORD BANK

Verbs (action words)			Nouns (people, places, things)		
explored	joined	visited	a book	a park	my brother
finished	made	won	a game	a story	the science club
helped	told		a painting	a video	

Hooray! Now you can tell about things you did in the past.
Tell your partner two things you did last week: *Last week,*
I (past-tense verb) (noun). I also (past-tense verb) (noun).

How I Feel

How do you feel? You might feel happy, proud, or another emotion. Let's learn how to talk about our emotions!

 ## Vocabulary Builder

1. Say It   **2.** See It   **3.** Read It   **4.** Write It

afraid

a • **fraid**
(adjective)

He is **afraid** of spiders.

Word _____
     afraid
Translation _____

Make Connections _____

_____

angry

an • gry
(adjective)

The two friends are **angry** with each other.

Word _____
     angry
Translation _____

Make Connections _____

_____

confused

con • **fused**
(adjective)

I was **confused** by the math homework.

Word _____
      confused

Translation _____

Make Connections _____

_____

embarrassed

em • **bar** • rassed
(adjective)

Jean was **embarrassed** after he fell.

Word _____
      embarrassed

Translation _____

Make Connections _____

_____

happy

hap • py
(adjective)

She is **happy** because she is winning the game.

Word _____
      happy

Translation _____

Make Connections _____

_____

Vocabulary and Language

nervous

nerv • ous
(adjective)

I felt **nervous** before starting a new job.

Word _____
nervous

Translation _____

Make Connections _____

_____

proud

proud
(adjective)

My mom felt **proud** when I graduated.

Word _____
proud

Translation _____

Make Connections _____

_____

sad

sad
(adjective)

She was **sad** when her friend moved away.

Word _____
sad

Translation _____

Make Connections _____

_____

Vocabulary Review

afraid	confused	happy	proud
angry	embarrassed	nervous	sad

Share translations with a partner.

> **LANGUAGE TO**
> **SHARE TRANSLATIONS**
>
> Can you share a word in (language)?
>
> The (language) word for _____ is _____.

Write sentences using new vocabulary.

1. When I am **confused** at school, I ask _____
   (Name)

   for help.

2. I feel **happy** when I _____.
   (verb phrase)

3. I feel **proud** when I _____.
   (verb phrase)

> **LANGUAGE TO**
> **SHARE IDEAS**
>
> What did you write?
>
> I wrote _____.

Language Builder

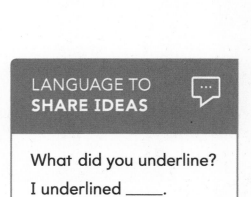

Adjectives for Emotions

Adjectives are words that **describe** a noun—a person, place, thing, or idea.

Adjectives can also describe a pronoun, such as *he*, *she*, or *they*.

Some **adjectives** tell about emotions.

happy	*confused*
sad	*embarrassed*

> Use <u>when</u> to tell what causes an emotion.
>
> *I feel **sad** <u>when</u> I lose a soccer game.*
> *They feel **happy** <u>when</u> they win a soccer game.*

<u>Underline</u> the adjectives that describe emotions.

Model: Sol is <u>proud</u> of her sister when she makes art.

1. I feel happy when I go to the park.

2. Cleo feels excited when she goes to a concert.

3. They feel confused when the questions on a test are difficult.

LANGUAGE TO SHARE IDEAS 💬

What did you underline?

I underlined _____.

Write an adjective to complete each sentence.

Model: I feel ___sad___ when my dog is sick.
(adjective)

1. His mom feels _____ when he gets good grades.
(adjective)

2. Esther feels _____ when she sees a snake.
(adjective)

3. I feel _____ when people smile at me.
(adjective)

WORD BANK 🧩

Adjectives (describing words)

afraid	happy
angry	nervous
confused	proud
embarrassed	sad

LANGUAGE TO SHARE IDEAS 💬

What did you write?

I wrote _____.

 **Listen Up**

Listen to the conversation.

▶ Hi, Mateo! What makes you feel happy?

Hello, Serene! I feel happy when I watch sports.

Nice! What makes you feel proud?

I feel proud when I speak English.

Talk About It

Partner A, ask questions. Partner B, respond. Then switch roles.

A: Hi, _____!
     (Name)

How do you feel when you win a game?

B: Hello, _____.
      (Name)

I feel _____ when I win a game.
     (adjective)

A: Nice! How do you feel when you meet a new friend?

B: I feel _____ when I meet a new friend.
     (adjective)

WORD BANK

Adjectives (describing words)

afraid	embarrassed	proud
angry	happy	sad
confused	nervous	

Text Type: Science Article

A **science article** tells about a science topic. Some science articles are **explanatory texts**. An explanatory text explains how to do something.

Explanatory texts often have features like **lists** and **examples**.

Excerpt from
5 Ways to Know Your Feelings Better

by Lisa M. Buckloh, PhD

1   Before you read on, take a moment to pause. Close your eyes if you want to and take a couple of calm breaths. Then ask yourself—how are you feeling right now?

2   Think of one-word answers that describe how you feel.

3   Notice what words come to mind. Does one feeling stand out? Or are there a few? You might even have opposite feelings at the same time. For example, **excited** and **nervous**. That's normal.

4   Just notice the emotions you feel at the moment. There's no right or wrong answer.

5   Doing this is a simple way to be aware of your emotions.

6   Sometimes it's easy to be **aware** of your emotions. Maybe there's one feeling that's strong and obvious to you. Other times, you might not pay much attention to how you feel. But your emotions are there. And they're all normal. Feelings are signals from the body that help us understand ourselves and make good decisions. For example, feeling *fear* in a situation like crossing the street in traffic is a useful signal to stay safe.

7   Being more aware of your emotions is a skill that can help you:

- know yourself better
- feel better about things and cope better
- be less self-critical
- pause instead of act on difficult emotions
- decide how to act and handle situations
- get along better with others

Glossary

....

aware (adjective)
When you are *aware* of something, you know it is happening.

opposite (adjective)
When two things are *opposite* of one another, they are very different. Happy and sad are *opposite* feelings.

8   Here are three ways to practice being more aware of your emotions:

1. <u>Notice and name your feelings</u>. To start, just notice how you feel as things happen. Say the name of the feeling to yourself. You might feel **proud** when something goes well. Or **disappointed** if you don't do well on a test. You might feel *relaxed* when sitting with friends at lunch. Or *nervous* before a test.

2. <u>Learn new words for feelings</u>. How many feeling words can you name? Try to think of even more. How many words are there for **angry**? For example, you might be *annoyed*, *upset*, or *mad*. You might be **irate**, **fuming**, or **outraged**.

3. <u>Keep a feelings journal</u>. Take a few minutes each day to write about how you feel and why. Writing about your feelings helps you get to know them better. Make art, write poetry, or compose music to express an emotion you feel.

9   Take time to get to know your emotions better. Just notice how you feel. Accept how you feel without judging yourself. Show yourself some kindness.

10   Remind yourself that all your emotions are normal. But how you act on emotions matters a lot. When you know your emotions, you're better able to make wise choices about how to act—no matter what you're feeling.

11   If you have emotions that feel difficult or overwhelming, get support. An adult you trust can help you talk through any tough feelings you're dealing with. Sometimes people get help from a therapist to deal with difficult emotions that affect daily life.

Glossary

disappointed (adjective)
When you feel ***disappointed***, you feel sad that something did not happen.

irate (adjective)
When you are ***irate***, you feel angry and annoyed by something.

fuming (adjective)
When you are ***fuming***, you feel very angry about something.

outraged (adjective)
When you are ***outraged***, you are extremely angry about something.

Take notes on the article.

_____

_____

_____

_____

LANGUAGE TO REACT

What is one thing you learned from the article?

One thing I learned is that _____.

· ·

What question do you have about the article?

One question I have is: _____?

Read and Respond

Text Feature: List

Authors use **text features** to organize information in an explanatory text.

A **list** is one type of text feature. An author might use a list to give important information in a simple way or to explain the steps in a process.

Lists often:

- Start with a statement that introduces the list and ends with a **colon**

- Use **bullet points** or **numbers** at the beginning of each item

- Include items that are a phrase, sentence, or paragraph

Read the text again. Draw a box around the lists.
Then answer the questions about the text.

1. Read this excerpt from the text.

"Feelings are signals from the body that help us understand
ourselves and make good decisions. For example, feeling fear
in a situation like crossing the street in traffic is a useful signal
to stay safe."

Based on the text, a good decision that feelings can help
us make is _____.

- (**a**) to stay inside

- (**b**) to walk to nearby places

- (**c**) to not cross the street in traffic

2. Read this excerpt from the text.

"Take a few minutes each day to write about how you feel and why.
Writing about your feelings helps you get to know them better. Make
art, write poetry, or compose music to express an emotion you feel."

Which sentence lists three examples for expressing your emotions?

- (**a**) the first sentence

- (**b**) the second sentence

- (**c**) the third sentence

Write About It

> **Remember!**
>
> Use the phrase **I feel (<u>adjective</u>) when** to share your emotions.
>
> *I feel <u>excited</u> when my favorite basketball team wins.*
>
> *I feel <u>nervous</u> when I have a test.*

WORD BANK

Adjectives (describing words)

afraid	happy
angry	nervous
confused	proud
embarrassed	sad

Write sentences about how you feel.

Model: How do you feel when you win an award?

I feel _____proud_____ when I win an award.
(adjective)

1. How do you feel when you get a gift?

   I feel _____ when I get a gift.
   (adjective)

2. How do you feel when you don't understand something?

   I feel _____ when I don't understand something.
   (adjective)

3. How do you feel when you see a big spider?

   I feel _____.
   (adjective . . .)

4. How do you feel when you make a mistake?

   I feel _____.
   (adjective . . .)

5. How do you feel when you have an argument?

   I feel _____.
   (adjective . . .)

Amazing! Now you can share your emotions with a friend. Tell your partner when you feel happy: *I feel happy when I (verb phrase).*

Sharing Memories

Last week, I played a new video game! What did you do last week? Let's learn how to share our memories—or talk about the things we've done in the past.

Vocabulary Builder

1. Say It   **2.** See It   **3.** Read It   **4.** Write It

---

winter

win • ter
(noun)

In the **winter**, it is cold and it snows.

Word _____
    winter

Translation _____

Make Connections _____

_____

---

spring

spring
(noun)

In the **spring**, it gets warmer.

Word _____
    spring

Translation _____

Make Connections _____

_____

---

summer

sum • mer
(noun)

In the **summer**, it gets hot.

Word _____
    summer

Translation _____

Make Connections _____

_____

fall

fall
(noun)

In the **fall**, it starts to get colder again.

Word _____
    fall

Translation _____

Make Connections _____

_____

vacation

va • **ca** • tion
(noun)

We went to a beach on our **vacation**.

Word _____
    vacation

Translation _____

Make Connections _____

_____

Vocabulary and Language

fun

fun
(adjective)

Playing video games with my cousin was **fun**.

Word _____
   fun

Translation _____

Make Connections _____

_____

special

spe • cial
(adjective)

When I won the prize, it was a **special** day for me.

Word _____
   special

Translation _____

Make Connections _____

_____

memory

mem • o • ry
(noun)

Old photos can make you think of **memories**—or things you did in the past.

Word _____
   memory

Translation _____

Make Connections _____

_____

Vocabulary Review

winter	summer	vacation	special
spring	fall	fun	memory

Share translations with a partner.

What happens in each season?

Winter (December, January, February)

- _____

- _____

Spring (March, April, May)

- _____

- _____

Summer (June, July, August)

- _____

- _____

Fall (September, October, November)

- _____

- _____

> **LANGUAGE TO SHARE TRANSLATIONS** 💬
>
> Can you share a word in (language)?
>
> The (language) word for _____ is _____.

> **LANGUAGE TO SHARE IDEAS** 💬
>
> What did you write?
>
> I wrote _____.
>
> •
>
> What else did you write?
>
> I also wrote _____.

Language Builder

Words to Describe When

Some words tell when something happened in the past.

Use **yesterday** to tell when something happened the day before today.

> **Yesterday**, we went to the library.
> We went to the library **yesterday**.

Use **last** to tell when something happened further back in the past.

> **Last week**, I had a math test.
> I had a math test **last week**.

> **Last year**, I went to a different school.
> I went to a different school **last year**.

Use a **comma** after **yesterday** or **last week/month/year** when the word or phrase is at the beginning of a sentence.

<u>Underline</u> the word or phrase that tells when the event happened.
Then rewrite the sentence by writing the word or phrase at the beginning.

Model: Yohan went to music class <u>yesterday</u>.

<u>Yesterday</u>, Yohan went to music class.

1. Yohan played video games last week.

_____, Yohan played video games.

2. Yohan spent time with his friends last Friday.

_____, Yohan spent time with his friends.

3. Yohan learned how to ride a bike last spring.

_____, Yohan learned how to ride a bike.

4. Yohan helped me clean up this morning.

_____, Yohan helped me clean up.

5. Yohan went to the beach last summer.

_____, Yohan went to the beach.

Listen Up

Listen to the conversation.

 Hi, Maria! What did you do last summer?

Last summer, I tried to play guitar.

That sounds fun. What did you do last winter?

Last winter, I hung out with friends.

Talk About It

Partner A, ask questions. Partner B, respond. Then switch roles.

A: Hi, _____!
   (Name)

What did you do _____?
               (words to describe when)

B: _____, I _____
   (Words to describe when)   (past-tense verb phrase)

_____.

A: Fun! What did you do _____?
                       (words to describe when)

B: _____, I _____
   (Words to describe when)   (past-tense verb phrase)

_____.

WORD BANK

Words to Describe When		Verb Phrases (action phrases)	
yesterday	winter	cooked dinner	studied English
last	spring	joined a club	watched a movie
week	summer	played soccer	went to the park
month	fall		
year			

Listen and Respond

Listen to the story and look at the pictures. Then take notes.

Event 1: Before the game, I was so _____
(adjective)

about playing. My friends and I sat quietly on the bench as we

_____ to start the game.
(past-tense verb)

Event 2: During the game, we worked together to score a goal!

When I _____ the ball past the goalie,
(past-tense verb)

I was so _____!
(adjective)

Event 3: After the game, we _____ together,
(past-tense verb)

and I felt _____ of myself and my teammates.
(adjective)

WORD BANK

Adjectives (describing words)	**Verbs (action words)**
happy nervous proud	celebrated kicked waited

Answer the questions.

1. What is the story about?

   (a) a new job

   (b) a rainy day

   (c) a special memory

2. When did the story happen?

   (a) last winter

   (b) last spring

   (c) last summer

   (d) last fall

3. At the end of the story, why is Maggie proud of herself and her team?

   (a) They won the game.

   (b) They stayed outside.

   (c) They made new friends.

Write About It

>  **Don't Forget!**
>
> You can use **yesterday** and **last** to tell about past events.
>
> > ***Yesterday**, we painted in art class.*
> >
> > ***Last spring**, we joined the drama club.*
> >
> > *We played in the snow **last winter**.*

What are some memories you have of times at school or with friends?

Memory	When

WORD BANK

Verbs (action words)

created	planted
explored	played
hung out	watched
learned	went to

_____

Words to Describe When

yesterday	winter
last	spring
week	summer
month	fall
year	

LANGUAGE TO SHARE IDEAS

What did you write?

I wrote ____.

Write About It

Write about memories of fun times at school.

Model: One memory I have of a fun time at school is when we <u>went to the library</u> <u>last fall</u>. Another memory I have is when we <u>built a robot in science class</u> <u>last week</u>.

One memory I have of a fun time at school is when we _____
(past-tense verb phrase)

_____

_____. Another memory I have is when
(words to describe when)

we _____
(past-tense verb phrase)

_____ .
(words to describe when)

WORD BANK

Verb Phrases (action phrases)	**Words to Describe When**	
created a video	yesterday	winter
explored a park	last	spring
hung out with friends	week	summer
learned something new	month	fall
planted a garden	year	
played volleyball		
watched a movie		
went on a field trip		

Write about memories of fun times with friends.

One memory I have of a fun time with friends is when we _____

(past-tense verb phrase)

_____

_____. Another memory I have is when

(words to describe when)

we _____

(past-tense verb phrase)

_____

_____.

(words to describe when)

Great job! Now you can share your memories. Tell your partner something you did in the past: *Last (week/month/year), I (past-tense verb phrase)*.

Setting the Scene

We go places every day! We go to school. Sometimes we go to a park. We might even go to a game! Let's learn how to describe the places where we go.

 ## Vocabulary Builder

1. Say It   **2.** See It   **3.** Read It   **4.** Write It

information

in • for • ma • tion
(noun)

Information is what you learn about a subject.

Word _____
          information

Translation _____

Make Connections _____

_____

sense

sense
(noun)

Our brain can get information through the five **senses**. A person can use their eyes, ears, nose, mouth, and the rest of their body to learn about the world around them.

Word _____
          sense

Translation _____

Make Connections _____

_____

see/sight

see/sight
(verb/noun)

Some people **see** with their eyes.
The sense of **sight** is the ability to see.

Word _____
        see/sight

Translation _____

Make Connections _____

_____

hear/hearing

hear/**hear** • ing
(verb/noun)

Some people **hear** with their ears.
The sense of **hearing** is the ability to hear.

Word _____
        hear/hearing

Translation _____

Make Connections _____

_____

smell

smell
(verb/noun)

Some people **smell** with their nose.
The sense of **smell** is the ability to smell.

Word _____
        smell

Translation _____

Make Connections _____

_____

taste

taste
(verb/noun)

Some people **taste** food with their mouth.
The sense of **taste** is the ability to taste.

Word _____
　　　taste

Translation _____

Make Connections _____

_____

touch

touch
(verb/noun)

When you **touch** an object, you learn how it feels.
The sense of **touch** is the ability to feel or touch something.

Word _____
　　　touch

Translation _____

Make Connections _____

_____

describe

de • **scribe**
(verb)

When you **describe** something, you tell what it looks, sounds, smells, tastes, or feels like.

Word _____
　　　describe

Translation _____

Make Connections _____

_____

Vocabulary Review

| information | see/sight | smell | touch |
| sense | hear/hearing | taste | describe |

Share translations with a partner.

> **LANGUAGE TO SHARE TRANSLATIONS**
>
> Can you share a word in (language)?
>
> The (language) word for _____ is _____.

Describe your classroom using any two of the five senses.

1. I see _____.

2. I hear _____.

3. I smell _____.

4. I taste _____.

5. I feel _____.

> **LANGUAGE TO SHARE IDEAS**
>
> What did you write?
>
> I wrote _____.

Language Builder

Adjectives and the Five Senses

Adjectives are describing words. We use **adjectives** to describe what we see, hear, smell, taste, and touch.

An **adjective** can come before the <u>noun</u> in a sentence.

*I see a **beautiful** <u>flower</u>.*
*I hear a **loud** <u>noise</u>.*

An **adjective** can come after the <u>noun</u> when there is a verb between them.

*The <u>bread</u> **smells** delicious.*
*The <u>soup</u> tastes **salty**.*
*The <u>water</u> is **cold**.*

Read the adjectives.

ADJECTIVES	
Sense	**Adjectives**
sight	beautiful, bright, colorful, dark
hearing	loud, noisy, quiet, soft
smell	delicious, fragrant, fresh, stinky
taste	juicy, salty, sour, spicy, sweet
touch	bumpy, cold, hot, rough, smooth

Match the sentence with the sense being described.

The cafeteria was stinky.

The courtyard was quiet.

The pool was cold.

The science lab was bright.

The air by the beach was salty.

touch

sight

taste

hearing

smell

LANGUAGE TO SHARE IDEAS

What did you match?

I matched _____ with _____.

Listen Up

Listen to the conversation.

▶ Hi, Taikhira! What senses can you use to describe a place?

Hello! I can use senses like sight and sound.

What do you mean?

I can use sight to describe what I see and sound to describe what I hear.

Talk About It

Partner A, **ask questions.** Partner B, **respond. Then switch roles.**

A: Hi, _____!
   (Name)

   What is one sense you can use to describe a place?

B: Hello, _____!
   (Name)

   I can use the sense of _____ to
   (sense)

   describe a place.

A: What do you mean?

B: I can use _____ to describe what
   (sense)

   I _____.
   (verb)

WORD BANK			🧩
Senses		**Verbs (action words)**	
sight	taste	hear	taste
smell	touch	see	touch
sound		smell	

Make Observations

Look at the picture. Discuss what you see. Take notes to help you.

_____

_____

_____

_____

_____

WORD BANK

Adjectives (describing words)	Nouns (people, things)
bright	baskets
earthy	flowers
green	fruits
purple	person
red	shoes
smooth	tomatoes
sweet	vegetables
tangy	
yellow	

LANGUAGE TO OBSERVE

What do you see?

I see ____.

· ·

What else do you see?

I also see ____.

Read and Respond

Read the text. Then describe a tomato.

Your **senses** help you understand the world around you. Imagine you are at a farmers' market. You can use your **senses** to determine if a tomato is ripe, or ready to eat. Don't hold the tomato up to your ear. There is nothing to **hear**! Look at the color of the tomato. Is it bright red, bright yellow, or deep purple? Does its skin feel firm? Does it **smell** earthy? Are the answers yes, yes, and yes? Then it's probably ripe! It will **taste** tangy and sweet. Your five **senses** can help you pick the perfect tomato—and do so much more!

Use the five senses to describe a tomato.

Sight: _____
  (adjective)

Touch: _____
  (adjective)

Smell: _____
  (adjective)

Taste: _____ and _____
  (adjective)   *(adjective)*

Sound: _____

LANGUAGE TO SHARE IDEAS 💬

What did you write?

I wrote _____.

Write About It

> **Remember!**
>
> Describe a place using **adjectives** that relate to the five senses: sight, sound, smell, taste, touch.
>
> *The library looked **crowded**.*
>
> *The cafeteria smelled **delicious**.*

Think about the last time you were at your favorite place. Write sentences to describe the place.

Model:

The <u>park</u> was <u>loud</u>.

The <u>park</u> felt <u>hot</u>.

The <u>park</u> <u>smelled</u> <u>clean</u>.

1. The _____ was _____.
   (noun)   (adjective)

2. The _____ was _____.
   (noun)   (adjective)

3. The _____   _____
   (noun)   (verb)

   _____.
   (adjective)

4. The _____   _____
   (noun)   (verb)

   _____.
   (adjective)

WORD BANK

Nouns (places)	Verbs (action words)	Adjectives (describing words)
basketball court	looked	beautiful
cafeteria	sounded	cold
library	smelled	hot
park	tasted	loud
school	felt	quiet
soccer field		

LANGUAGE TO SHARE IDEAS

What did you write?

I wrote _____.

Fantastic! Now you can describe a place. Tell your partner about your favorite place: *My favorite place is (noun). It is (adjective) and (adjective).*

Write a Personal Narrative

Now that you've learned how to talk about yourself, you can write a personal narrative—or a true story about yourself.

 ## View a Student Model

Read this comic strip created by a student.

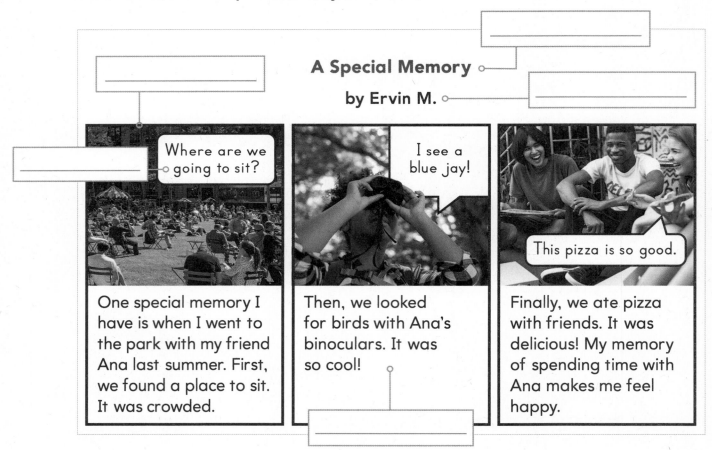

Label the parts of the comic strip.

| title | author | panel | caption | speech bubble |

Create a comic strip to tell a story about a memory.
Use past-tense verbs and adjectives to tell the story.

 ## Mark Elements

Read the student model. Mark the elements.

A Special Memory

by Ervin M.

One special memory I have is when I went to the park with my friend Ana last summer. First, we found a place to sit. It was crowded. Then, we looked for birds with Ana's binoculars. It was so cool! Finally, we ate pizza with friends. It was delicious! My memory of spending time with Ana makes me feel happy.

1. In the introductory sentence, <u>underline</u> the where, who, and when from the story.

2. The story has a beginning, middle, and end. Each section tells about an event. Draw a box around the word that signals each event.

3. <u>Underline</u> the concluding sentence.

4. Highlight in yellow the past-tense verbs, or action words.

5. Highlight in green the adjectives.

Project Prompt

Create a comic strip to tell a story about a memory.
Use past-tense verbs and adjectives to tell the story.

 Brainstorm Ideas

What are some of your special memories?

Memories from School	Memories from Outside of School
• played volleyball in P.E. class with Noelia	• went to the science center with Erick
•	•
•	•

LANGUAGE TO SHARE IDEAS

What did you write?

I wrote _____.

Review Vocabulary

Identify words or phrases from the unit to use in your writing.

Past-Tense Verbs	Adjectives for Places

Adjectives for Emotions	Words to Describe When

LANGUAGE TO COLLABORATE 💬

What can we write?

We can write _____.

Write Together

Write the story of a special memory with a friend at school.

1. Brainstorm: Where, When, Who

Where does the story take place? _____
(place)

When does the story happen? _____
(when)

Who are the main characters? Me, _____
(Name of Friend)

2. Write the introductory sentence.

Title: A Special Memory

Introductory sentence: One special memory I have is when I went to

_____ with my friend
(place)

_____   _____ .
(Name)   (when)

3. Outline the story.

First Event	Second Event	Third Event

Write Together

4. Draft the story.

Title: _____
   (Title)

   One special memory I have is when I went to _____
                                               (place)

with my friend _____
               (Name)

_____.
(when)

First, we _____.
         (past-tense verb phrase)

It was _____.
       (adjective)

Then, we _____.
         (past-tense verb phrase)

It was _____.
       (adjective)

Finally, we _____.
            (past-tense verb phrase)

It was _____!
       (adjective)

My memory of spending time with _____
                                (Name)

makes me feel _____.
              (adjective)

Write With a Partner

Write the story of a special memory with a friend.

1. Brainstorm: Where, When, Who

Where does the story take place? _____
(place)

When does the story happen? _____
(when)

Who are the main characters? Me, _____
(Name of Friend)

2. Write the introductory sentence.

Title: A Special Memory

Introductory sentence: One special memory I have is when I went to

_____ with my friend
(place)

_____   _____.
(Name)   *(when)*

3. Outline the story.

First Event	Second Event	Third Event

Write With a Partner

4. Draft the story.

Title: _____
        (Title)

One special memory I have is when I went to _____
                                                    (place)

with my friend _____   _____.
              (Name)   _(when)_

First, we _____.
        (past-tense verb phrase)

It was _____.
      (adjective)

Then, we _____.
        (past-tense verb phrase)

It was _____.
      (adjective)

Finally, we _____.
          (past-tense verb phrase)

It was _____!
      (adjective)

My memory of spending time with _____
                                (Name)

makes me feel _____.
            (adjective)

> **LANGUAGE TO COLLABORATE**
>
> What can we write?
>
> We can write _____.

Project Prompt

Create a comic strip to tell a story about a memory.
Use past-tense verbs and adjectives to tell the story.

 ## Choose a Prompt

Select a task for your project:

☐ a memory from school

☐ a memory from outside of school

LANGUAGE TO SHARE IDEAS

What did you choose?

I chose _____.

 ## Write the Story Elements

Brainstorm the elements of the story.

Where does the story take place?

_____
(place)

When does the story happen?

_____
(when)

Who are the main characters?

Me, _____
(Name of Friend)

Outline the Story

Outline the story.

First Event	Second Event	Third Event

Draft a Paragraph

Draft the story.

Title: _____
(title)

    One special memory I have is when I went to _____
(place)

with my friend _____
(Name)

_____.
(when)

First, we _____.
(past-tense verb phrase)

It was _____.
(adjective)

Then, we _____.
(past-tense verb phrase)

It was _____.
(adjective)

Finally, we _____.
(past-tense verb phrase)

It was _____!
(adjective)

My memory of spending time with _____
(Name)

makes me feel _____.
(adjective)

Check and Edit

Use this checklist to review and edit your draft.

Did you . . .

- ☐ include where, who, and when in the introductory sentence?

- ☐ write the beginning, middle, and end of the story in the correct order?

- ☐ use past-tense verbs to tell what happened?

- ☐ use adjectives to describe events?

- ☐ spell vocabulary words correctly?

 ## Create a Comic Strip

Choose your final project format. Then create your comic strip.

☐ Paper Comic Strip	☐ Digital Comic Strip
1. Write the events on paper. 2. Add images by drawing or cutting and pasting pictures.	1. Type the events on the computer. 2. Add images by searching online or taking pictures and uploading them.
Optional: Make it multilingual by adding translations.	

Engage Your Audience

When you present ideas during class, **engage your audience**.

- Turn toward your audience so that they know you are ready to present.

- Look up from your notes every few seconds to engage your listeners.

Partner Practice

Share your comic strip with a partner. Then switch roles.

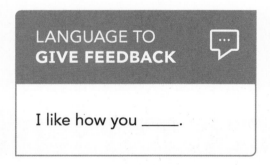

LANGUAGE TO GIVE FEEDBACK

I like how you _____.

WORD BANK

Feedback

turned toward me

spoke loudly

looked up

Present Comic Strips

Share your comic strip with the group or class.
Engage your audience.

Listen and Take Notes

Listen to your classmates and take notes on their stories.

Classmate's Name	Story Elements (Where, When, Who)

 ## Reflect

Write one way you can improve your next presentation.

One way I can improve my next presentation is to _____

_____ .

WORD BANK

Verb Phrases (action phrases)

turn toward the audience   speak louder

look up more often   practice more

You did it! You finished Unit 2 and learned all about sharing your interests and connecting with others. Way to go!

Language Expectations and Goals

Unit 2: Getting to Know You

Before each lesson, preview the lesson goals. When you complete a lesson, mark the box ☑ next to each goal you reached.

Lesson 1	Getting to Know You

☐ I can watch a video to learn about making friends.

☐ I can name the characters from the video.

☐ I can take notes on a video using new words.

☐ I can ask and answer questions about interests.

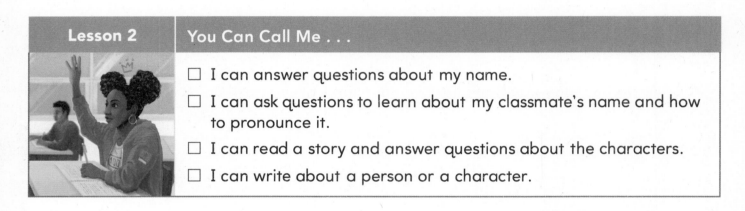

Lesson 2	You Can Call Me . . .

☐ I can answer questions about my name.

☐ I can ask questions to learn about my classmate's name and how to pronounce it.

☐ I can read a story and answer questions about the characters.

☐ I can write about a person or a character.

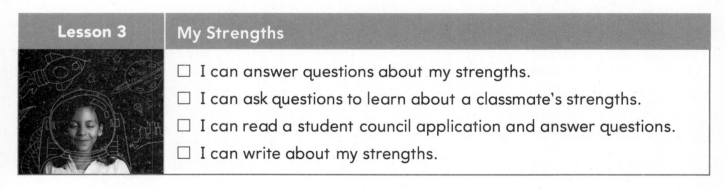

Lesson 3	My Strengths

☐ I can answer questions about my strengths.

☐ I can ask questions to learn about a classmate's strengths.

☐ I can read a student council application and answer questions.

☐ I can write about my strengths.

Lesson 4	Save the Date
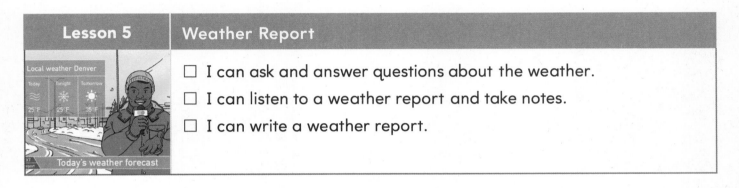	☐ I can ask and answer questions about important dates. ☐ I can read a calendar and answer questions about events. ☐ I can write about dates and events.

Lesson 5	Weather Report
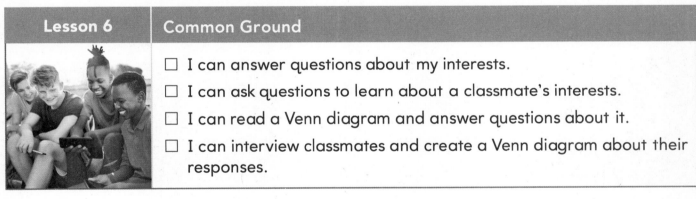	☐ I can ask and answer questions about the weather. ☐ I can listen to a weather report and take notes. ☐ I can write a weather report.

Lesson 6	Common Ground
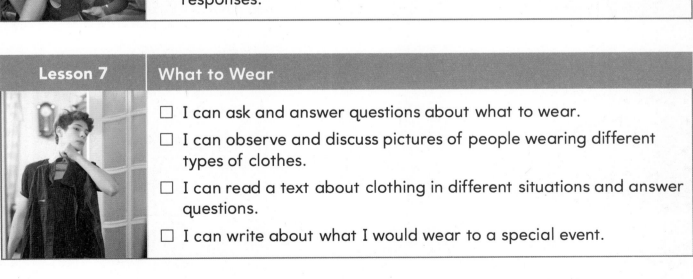	☐ I can answer questions about my interests. ☐ I can ask questions to learn about a classmate's interests. ☐ I can read a Venn diagram and answer questions about it. ☐ I can interview classmates and create a Venn diagram about their responses.

Lesson 7	What to Wear
	☐ I can ask and answer questions about what to wear. ☐ I can observe and discuss pictures of people wearing different types of clothes. ☐ I can read a text about clothing in different situations and answer questions. ☐ I can write about what I would wear to a special event.

Language Expectations and Goals

Lesson 8	Everyday Habits

☐ I can ask and answer questions about my habits.

☐ I can observe and discuss pictures showing a student's habits.

☐ I can read a text about a student's habits and answer questions.

☐ I can write about my habits.

Lesson 9	A Day in My Life

☐ I can answer questions about my daily activities.

☐ I can ask questions to learn about a classmate's daily activities.

☐ I can read a pie chart and answer questions.

☐ I can create a pie chart and write about it.

Lesson 10	Catching Up

☐ I can answer questions about what I did yesterday.

☐ I can ask questions to learn about what a classmate did yesterday.

☐ I can read an email and answer questions.

☐ I can write an email to a friend.

Lesson 11	How I Feel

☐ I can ask and answer questions about feelings.

☐ I can read an explanatory text and answer questions.

☐ I can write about feelings.

Lesson 12	Sharing Memories
	☐ I can answer questions about memories.
	☐ I can ask questions to learn about a classmate's memories.
	☐ I can listen to a student's story and take notes.
	☐ I can write about a memory.

Lesson 13	Setting the Scene
	☐ I can ask and answer questions about the five senses.
	☐ I can observe and discuss a picture of a place.
	☐ I can read a text about using the five senses and write about an object from the text.
	☐ I can write about a special place.

Lesson 14	Project: Write a Personal Narrative
	☐ I can mark the parts of a narrative text.
	☐ I can write a story about a memory.
	☐ I can check and edit my writing.
	☐ I can create a comic strip and engage my audience when I present.

Unit Reflections

Since **Unit 1**, I think my skills have improved in:

☐ speaking   ☐ reading

☐ listening   ☐ writing

In **Unit 2**, I learned how to _____

_____.

Credits

Getting to Know You

arepas ©Zoonar GmbH/Alamy; *dolma* ©ld1976/Adobe Stock

You Can Call Me...

pointing to shirt ©Asier/Adobe Stock; *with great thought* ©Prostock-studio/Shutterstock; *teen facepalming* ©Daniel Ernst/Adobe Stock

My Strengths

student giving presentation ©Image Source/Getty Images; *working robotics* ©Hero Images/Getty Images; *boy using binoculars* ©MoMo Productions/DigitalVision/Getty Images; *students in class* ©fizkes/Shutterstock; *girl dreaming* ©Marilyn Nieves/E+/Getty Images; *boy helping mother* ©JAG Images/Corbis/Getty Images; *helping with homework* ©Maskot Images/Media Bakery; *girl doing homework* ©Odua Images/Shutterstock

Save the Date

hand with pen ©Piman Khrutmuang/Adobe Stock; *celebrating birthday* ©FG Trade/E+/Getty Images

Weather Report

weather icons ©lyeyee/Shutterstock; *groups of friends* ©anouchka/iStock/Getty Images; *umbrella* ©juliasudnitskaya/Adobe Stock; *boy with dog* ©Cavan Images/Getty Images; *windy day* ©Carol Yepes/Moment/Getty Images; *Temperature* ©N_studio/Adobe Stock; *thermometer - cold* ©Marian Weyo/Shutterstock; *thermometer - hot* ©Guenter Albers/Shutterstock

Common Ground

teen coding ©5432action/E+/Getty Images; *making dinner* ©miodrag ignjatovic/E+/Getty Images; *making pottery* ©Ann Kosolapova/Shutterstock; *teens dancing* ©Nick David/Stone/Getty Images; *artist* ©SDI Productions/E+/Getty Images; *riding bicycle* ©Nataliia/Adobe Stock; *choir* ©Monkey Business Images/Shutterstock; *friends* ©AJ_Watt/E+/Getty Images

What to Wear

trying on clothes ©Mike_shots/Shutterstock; color wheel ©Imagewriter/Adobe Stock; *teen wearing sunglasses* ©Zivica Kerkez/Shutterstock; *woman in street* ©Francisco Rodriguez Herna/Shutterstock; *man in raincoat* ©RyanJLane/E+/Getty Images; *tying shoes* ©Maskot/Getty Images; *boy with glasses* ©DisobeyArt/Adobe Stock; *redheaded boy* ©Seventyfour/Adobe Stock; *boy in blizzard* ©Imgorthand/E+/Getty Images; *girl with sunglasses* ©Darren Baker/Dreamstime; *teenager in autumn* ©Just dance/Shutterstock; *siblings in winter* ©Adam and Kev/DigitalVision/Getty Images; *baseball players* ©PeopleImages.com - Yuri A/Shutterstock; *family at celebration* ©Thomas Barwick/Stone/Getty Images; *girl with phone* ©kucherav/Adobe Stock

A Day in My Life

working out ©Nanausop/Shutterstock; *artist* ©Pollyana Ventura/E+/Getty Images; *washing dishes* ©MoMo Productions/DigitalVision/Getty Images; *doing homework* ©SolStock/E+/Getty Images; *female pupil playing guitar* ©Monkey Business Images/Shutterstock; *students eating pizza* ©Rawpixel.com/Shutterstock; *supermarket employee* ©Photographerlondon/Dreamstime; *looking at watch* ©Have a nice day Photo/Shutterstock

Catching Up

girl with binoculars ©MISTER DIN/Shutterstock; *chore chart* ©John D. Buffington/Getty Images; *helping with homework* ©Monkey Business Images/Shutterstock; *group of students* ©sek_suwat/Shutterstock; *teenager vlogging* ©Xavier Lorenzo/Adobe Stock; *students talking* ©Sarah Fix/Blend Images - Moxie Productions/Getty Images; *children greeting grandparents* ©gahsoon/E+/Getty Images; *soccer team celebrating* ©Alistair Berg/DigitalVision/Getty Images

How I Feel

scared boy ©pathdoc/Shutterstock; *angry friends* ©praetorianphoto/E+/Getty Images; *tired student* ©Stokkete/Shutterstock; *embarrassed boy* ©MDV Edwards/Shutterstock; *wheelchair tennis* ©Kohei Hara/DigitalVision/Getty Images; *upset woman* ©damircudic/E+/Getty Images; *graduate* ©SDI Productions/E+/Getty Images; *sad girl* ©tommaso79/Shutterstock; *boy stares at homework* ©Jeff Hathaway/iStockPhoto.com

Sharing Memories

same tree depicting four seasons ©Mihai_Andritoiu/Shutterstock; *family taking pictures* ©kate_sept2004/E+/Getty Images; *playing video game* ©pololia/Adobe Stock; *girl with trophy* ©triloks/E+/Getty Images; *photo album* ©kate_sept2004/E+/Getty Images

Setting the Scene

brain ©Nazarii M/Shutterstock, *information* ©Vladgrin/Shutterstock, *five senses* ©Sudowoodo/Shutterstock; *teens looking at art* ©Philippe Lissac/Stone/Getty Images; *vegetable market* ©Madeleine Steinbach/Adobe Stock

Speaking and Listening characters

Santiago illustration adapted from ©HMH; *Serene illustration adapted from* ©Johner Images/Alamy; *Mateo illustration adapted from* ©HMH; *Shaun illustration adapted from* ©nuiiko/Adobe Stock; *Taikhira illustration adapted from* ©Silverblack/Dreamstime; *Chris illustration adapted from* ©Ajphotos/Dreamstime; *Maria illustration adapted from* ©digitalskillet/Getty Images